SHANA COWAN

LIFE BEYOND TODAY

*If You Don't Make Decisions, Decisions
Will Be Made For You*

Copyright © Shana Cowan

I dedicate this book to my mother,

Pearlie Holmes.

You inspired me to be the best version of myself. You taught me to never give up on anyone, even if it felt like you should!

God gives us back everything that man may have taken.

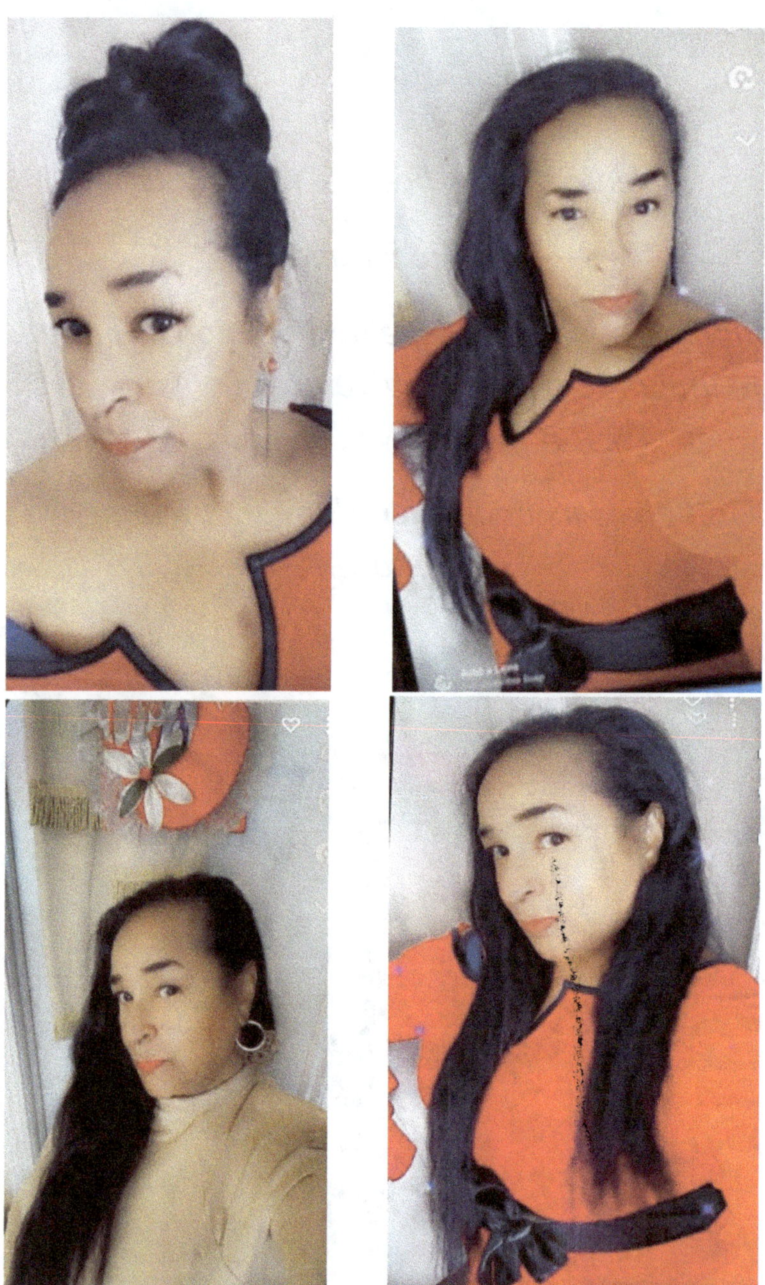

__About the Author__

Author Shana Cowan was born in Cocoa Beach, Florida but raised in Columbus, GA. She has a Bachelor's degree in criminal justice, a Master's in Education, and is a certified Paralegal. While she has always been successful in maintaining a comfortable life for her and her children, she always had a strong desire to help others. So she knew ultimately that she wanted to provide a service that would expand her reach and allow her to help on a grand scale. After experiencing the loss of someone close to her and witnessing the major lesson that accompanied that loss, her extensive knowledge and passion for helping became the foundation and core of her newly founded business Life Beyond Today LLC. While she has already achieved so much, this is just the beginning for Shana as a writer and a business owner. Look for much more to come!

Contents

A double-sided man is unstable in all his ways,
(James. 1:8) *if you do not make a decision, decisions
will be made for you. I am living proof the person I
loved didn't make the needed decisions, so I made the
decision for him. I chose to leave the relationship and
put my happiness first!*

INTRODUCTION

Release is the core purpose for this book. I am writing it to release what I've been holding in for so long and to tell my story. I've held things in for so many years to protect the images and the character of certain people, but I'm tired of looking out for the wellbeing of others. It's time for me to have my own back and do what's best for me! It's time for me to unload the burden of experiences that others inflicted on me and finally know what it feels like to have that weight lifted.

What's done in the dark will always come to light. Things that hurt should not be bottled up inside but released in order for healing and rebuilding to take place. I'm releasing it all into this book. Some things are kept private as respect to the children that were involved; but I'm putting all the rumors to bed, all the lies to shame, and releasing the truth. Things were done in the public eye, so why should I not address these things and set it all straight?

As I tell my story, I will bounce around because certain things need to be explained more than the order of the timeline needs to be kept. This book should be an eye opener for those who are not aware of what may be happening right under their nose. It's a warning to everyone to have their affairs in order now. Make those important decisions now or someone else will make them for you. I have never spoken on the things that happened to me publicly until now; and this will be the first and last time!

This is my story!

CHAPTER 1

The Start
Of
My Childhood

I grew up in a respectable middle-class household, being well taken care of with my two older brothers and younger sister. The opportunities of being on the cheerleading and dance teams, JROTC, and attending different summer programs and camps, made me feel like I had a good childhood.

During my younger years, my oldest brother strayed away as he left to live with his dad. My mother raised the rest of us on her own. She made sure we were in the church 24 /7, and it was something we became used to. In every Sunday bible school class, we recited the books of the bible like our ABC's. We were devout members in a local pastor's church all throughout my childhood in Columbus, Georgia and we followed the same pastor in my later years to Alabama.

From the audience looking into the pulpits, I admired the pastor and his preaching. His sermons were so on point, and I sought to one day marry a man just like him. Although I was young and had to grow to understand what he was preaching about, I was attentive at the sound of his voice. His words were so in tune. My fascination with the word of God was something I could never fully understand, but it was a magic that I never wanted to go away.

One day after speaking to my mother about church and how much I loved it, we began to get deeper into our conversation and exploring the passion I felt.

My father was never around, so I never really had a relationship with him… at least that's what I thought for a long time. Then, one day, between the ages of 10-12, my mother sat me down and revealed the identity of my father. I was at a loss for words! In my mind, I was thinking, "How could this be!?" As I sat under the pastor and listened to his sermons, all I could think was *'I need to go up to him and talk to him, since I did grow up in his church' he will hear me out*. My mother tried to explain to me that it wasn't that simple; but as a child, I couldn't understand what the big issue was. What was the problem with me going and talking to him myself, especially since this pastor is my father?

I can only assume that in the back of her mind, my mother probably knew that he wouldn't acknowledge me in any way. So, she tried to shield me from the pain of rejection. As a 10- to 12-year-old young girl, I failed to understand that what she was telling me was protection and warning.

A few Sundays later, during prayer service in Alabama, I went up to the pastor and handed him a school picture of myself. He accepted it. I felt so proud that I had a chance to give him one of the pictures I had taken in school. I'm not sure what he did with it; but as I went back to my seat, prayer service continued.

From this moment on, the conversation was no longer a topic that my mother and I discussed. It was just never spoken about but soon after, we moved away from the church where the man I learned to be my father was the pastor and we joined a new church.

As I grew older, I had more questions. I wanted to know how was the pastor of our old church my father and why he never acknowledged me as his child? My mother finally told me the story behind my existence. She explained to me that when I was conceived, she was in a broken space and had become very spiritual and *'caught up in the word'*. At that point, she committed herself to the church. She basically lived there… attended every service, every prayer night and revival. Anything the church may have needed, she was there to help.

While spending so much of her time at the church, she and the pastor became close. She hadn't been touched by a man in three years; and this man was so convincing. He was so accommodating. He used to call transportation for my mother to go and visit him at hotels. He made it easy to fall for his charms.

Eventually, he started to open up and tell her that he was no longer happy in his marriage. She would tell him to pray about it and God would work it out. From those encounters and that union, I was conceived. She said that it wasn't supposed to happen, but it did. Terminating her pregnancy was not even a thought. Sometime after she found out she was pregnant, the church went to visit another church. Many of the members rode together in the church van the pastor owned. My mother, unaware of how the plan came together, ended up on the van alone with the pastor's brother. She was young, vulnerable, and very much in a compromising position as she was only trying to do what she thought would be best for her baby. On the van, she was taken advantage of. She knew the pastor automatically knew what was going on. No one knew it yet but him, that she was already pregnant. The pastor was a very cunning man and was desperately trying to cover up what he had done to protect his ministry. After this happened, my mother decided to move away. She was hesitant but she knew it was the best decision at the time. The pastor was at the hospital when I was born, my mother said he was hoping something happened to her during childbirth because she was so sick at the time. The man was ruthless! With her leaving the church then later returning with a new baby, there were whispers about her in the pews and hallways of the church. People gossiped about how I looked and who my father could be. My mother told me that from the whispers, they all knew what had taken place. As a matter of fact, this pastor even came to see me in the hospital when I was born, so he knew that I was his child. When my mother returned to the church, no one could know why she moved or who my father was, reason being is because my father… the pastor… was married! Yes, you read that right…

He was married! I didn't know, even then, how that knowledge or my father's rejection would affect me.

In my high school years, I was the captain of the cheerleading team. I also participated in the band, chorus, and JROTC. While being active in school, I found time to squeeze in a part time job at Popeyes Chicken. That was where I met my ex-husband. He was working full time in the military. Of course, I wanted to be grown so I thought I was in love. We dated for a couple of years, then during my senior year of high school, I got pregnant. Shortly after, we got married.

My mother made sure I wouldn't become another statistic - not completing high school due to pregnancy. She hired a tutor to come to our home the days I couldn't make it to school. The principal of the high school tried to convince my mother to send me to a school for pregnant students. I could not conceive the thought of it and my mother shared the sentiment respond with a stiff "heck no". In May of 2000, I walked across the stage to graduate, five months pregnant.

Four months later, I gave birth to my beautiful, healthy son. Shortly after my son was born, I lost my grandmother. It was a very traumatic experience being a new mother and losing someone so close to me all at once. This same pastor spoke at my grandmother's funeral, and he was there to support the family.

A few years after our son was born, my then husband was deployed to Korea. Losing someone so close to you, having a new baby, then having your husband get deployed away all within a year was a lot to bare. Neither one of us was ready for marriage in the first place; so, holding things together while living apart was a lot to handle for both of us. Our relationship ended very quickly after he left the country; we separated in 2003. He moved back to his hometown of Florida when his term overseas was over and got out of the military. I got my own place and lived as a single woman with my son while bartending from 2003-2005 in Columbus, GA. It's funny. Only in hindsight can I see how fast life was unfolding and I still wasn't aware of how my choices were all connected to my past.

For years, I reached out to the pastor who was my father, but he never responded. Then one day I decided to send a text message, but his other daughters replied saying, **"he is not your dad so stop texting him!"** I was in disbelief… *like, WTF!!*

As a young woman, I needed answers… an explanation as to why he never acknowledged me as his child. This rejection left a void in my heart that only a conversation with him could fill. In so many ways, I needed him. I needed to hear his voice - again, just like when I sat in the pews during Sunday worship services as a young girl. I needed his side of my story to make sense of it all; but his other daughters made sure to keep us away from one another as they intercepted my phone calls. They eventually stopped answering my calls whenever I made attempts to contact and simply talk to him. I even reached out to him when he was sick, but they would send mean text messages in response.

There was already a wound from him not acknowledging me as his daughter throughout my childhood years, then to have his daughters (who he does claim) say the things they did, it cut me to the core. I was scarred and my feelings were all over the place. I wondered, *'if they knew I existed, why were they treating me like this?'* The circumstances of my existence may not have been right, but I was not to blame. I didn't deserve to get beat up with their words. Neither was there a need for them to make me feel bad. I am the product of their father's infidelity, a result of a choice he made – not a disease to be avoided or a mistake best to be forgotten. Still, instead of them holding him accountable or turning their anger and disappointment towards him, they aimed it at me.

Since his daughters were not open to having a decent conversation with me, years later, I reached out to his son. He and I talked for over a year's time, and he was shocked when I told him that his dad was also my father. I kind of felt like he had to know because like I said previously, I grew up in the church. He did agree to give me a DNA test, but he also said that he had to discuss it with his father. So, I gave him time and we kept in touch. We would talk often for a long period of time. Then one day in September of 2022, I reached out to ask if he was still open to doing the test with me. I even offered to pay for it, but he declined. He said that he had spoken to his father and out of respect for him, he couldn't do it.

Of course, I couldn't help but wonder, *'what's the big deal to get a test done if he feels like he wasn't my father?'* I guess he was afraid of the truth being unveiled. I digress. I told his son that I understood and left well enough alone. I also told myself that would be my last time reaching out in 2021. I'm not his judge or his maker, he has a higher God to answer to and that day is sure to come!

The Start Of My Childhood

The Start Of My Childhood

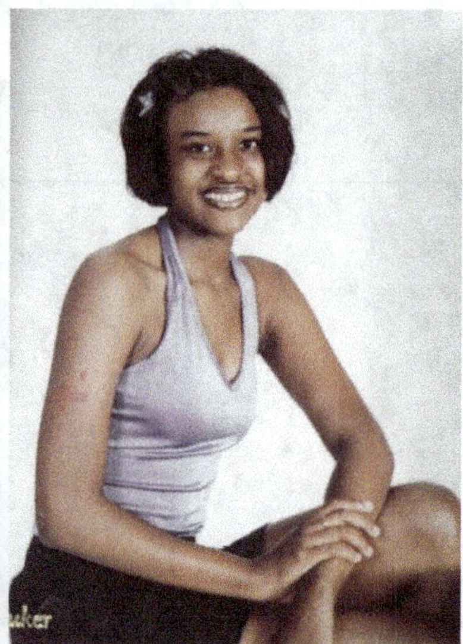

In 2005, with all the rejections I had experienced and the disappointment of my failing marriage, I was ready for a new beginning. I filed for divorce from my husband and headed for the big city - a fresh start in Atlanta! Despite my promise to myself that I wouldn't, I continued to reach out to the pastor but my attempts to talk to him were unsuccessful.

Finally, one day in 2006, he agreed to meet with me in Atlanta. Since his birthday had just passed, I presented him with a gift and a long letter that I wrote to him. I requested that he read it in front of me. After he read it, he was shocked. I basically revealed to him that I knew everything; but that I wasn't mad about the way he had handled things. I just wanted to get to know him, as my father. He said he would need time to think it over and get back with me. At that moment, I felt like if he had any doubt, that was the time to say it. He said nothing so I figured that there were no doubts in his mind that he is my father. The pastor knew the truth and the church people knew as well! His rejection had just been to protect his title and preserve his image. I wondered how a man of God could be okay with making those decisions, but I was open to giving him time to make his decision. I just prayed he made a better one than he had in the past.

I am his daughter!

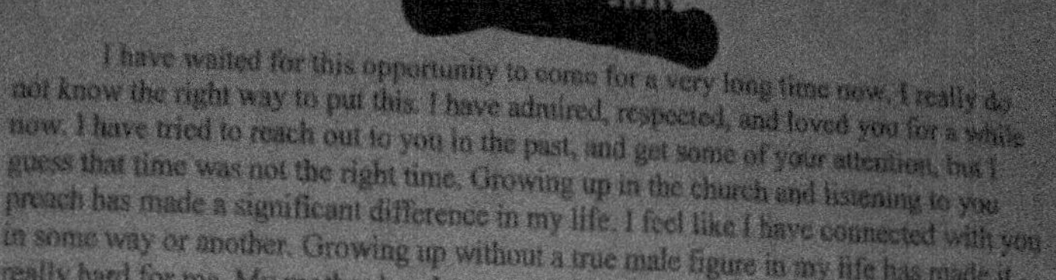

I have waited for this opportunity to come for a very long time now. I really do not know the right way to put this. I have admired, respected, and loved you for a while now. I have tried to reach out to you in the past, and get some of your attention, but I guess that time was not the right time. Growing up in the church and listening to you preach has made a significant difference in my life. I feel like I have connected with you in some way or another. Growing up without a true male figure in my life has made it really hard for me. My mother has done a great job raising me, but I have always felt that I needed the male figure to fill that void that I was missing.

I have always questioned my mother about the man who I believed was my father. After a while, she always sort of avoided answering any of my questions. Then I told her I felt a connection with you and that it felt weird. This is when she revealed to me that you were my father. I knew I always felt this way about you for a reason and with her telling me this, it confirmed why I have been feeling the way. I never said anything to you growing up because you were married and I didn't want to cause problems or push you further away from me. I am now a woman and I do want some kind of relationship with you. If right now isn't a good time for you, I will understand. But like you said in church, tomorrow is not promised and I don't want to leave this world without knowing what kind of father you are. I don't want to wait any longer not knowing whether you or I would live another day to see each other or spend time with one another.

This has been the hardest decision for me to ever have to make. I have held in my emotions for some time now. After seeing you in church, all my emotions came back. My mother has done a phenomenal job with me. I just wanted that father figure in my life, someone who really cared for me. I know you care about me but maybe you just were not ready at that particular time. I really hope after me coming to you and wanting a relationship with you, that you do not pull away from me. I need you now in my life more than I ever needed you before. I believe you're a great man of God and I just want this chance to get closer to you if you would allow me to. I admire you and someday I hope to be just like you. I have sinned and I know I need to get closer to God but I need to get closer to you as well. A piece of me have been missing for some time now and that missing piece was you. I need you in my life as a friend, a mentor, and my father.

I have prayed and wished for this day to come for sometime now. I am here now and I would love the chance for you to give me a chance to be your daughter. Growing up, I wish I'd had a father figure to come to with problems and issues I had. I would like you and I to just get to know one another, if this would be all right with you. Once we get together, I will be delighted to answer any questions you may have of me and I would like you to answer questions I may have about you. I hope this is a fresh start to a new beginning and a spectacular **father-daughter** relationship.

Love, Shana   I LOVE YOU DAD!

The Start Of My Childhood

The Beginning
Of Life
As Becoming
An Adult

After my big move to Atlanta, I started dating a guy name JB. We initially met in my hometown of Columbus, GA and dated on and off between 2006-2013. The relationship started off with us just linking up in Columbus, every now and then and grew over time. In Atlanta, I worked two jobs and got my own place. JB also had his own place, but it was in a very bad area living with his brother, so I opened my door and he decided to move in with me. HUGE MISTAKE. *Never move in with someone when you're not sure where you stand or will go with them in the future.*

In the beginning, the relationship was okay… it was just comfortable; but from the start I felt it would never excel past that. Shortly after he moved in with me, I got pregnant. I must admit that we really weren't trying to prevent pregnancy. I was just making mistake after mistake with him and it would take me on a downward spiral.

JB had some of his things there and I often used his desktop computer to work on things for school, resumes, etc. I noticed his son's mother's name in his computer and her last name happened to be the same as his. Of course, I questioned it and yep, you guessed it, THEY WERE MARRIED!

JB said the marriage was to legalize her since she wasn't a US citizen and that at the time, they were separated but his son would often visit. I asked him about his plans regarding divorce, since I felt he was just dragging it on; and he expressed that his only concern was being put on child support. In addition, he didn't want his son to have to move away because his mom was no longer allowed in the US. I didn't buy it; but since I was already pregnant, I just rolled with it when I should've run far away and I felt that in my soul.

After obtaining my bachelor's degree during my pregnancy, I decided to go back to school to earn my Master's - all while working two bartending jobs and raising 2 children. I also bought my first home in May of 2012.

JB loved hanging out and was always throwing parties and events at any moment. I honestly got tired of entertaining for every single event he wanted to host. His drinking was a major issue, and it didn't get any better. This relationship quickly became very toxic. He was both mentally and verbally abusive.

The majority of the time, he was cheating and doing what he wanted to do. Even though I didn't see a promising future with JB, I didn't want my daughter to grow up without her dad in her life. So, I stayed in the relationship.

The cheating never stopped, and the relationship wasn't going to grow any further until he was honest and true with himself. After a while I didn't care anymore, I just accepted things for how they were and he continued to do what he wanted to do. So, I began to match that energy! I knew it would get old fast and figured that's when we would address the issues at hand.

The last straw for me was him texting and making sexual advances towards someone I let stay in my home and watch over our daughter. To be clear, she never responded back to him or engaged; but that was it for me! I had to let the relationship go and think of my well-being and the well-being of my children because I didn't want my daughter or my son to see us arguing and fighting all the time.

I finally decided to put the relationship to an end and find some sort of happiness. Raising my children in peace was more important. Besides, the divorce never happened.

CHAPTER 3

BUILDING MY LIFE

A New Chapter

2013 – 2022

I Met Harry

In November 2013, my best friend, Lisa, and I went to Barnacle's sports bar in Decatur, Georgia. At the time, JB still had not moved out of the house yet, so I wasn't going out to meet anyone new. I just simply wanted to get away and relax with my friend. That night, we met a guy named Harry and he bought us a round of drinks. After enjoying an evening of music, food, and laughter, he asked for my number to keep in touch. For a while, we communicated via text. When he mentioned that he was going through a divorce and wasn't ready for anything serious, I admired his transparency. Besides, due to my home situation at the time, I wasn't in position to be searching for anything or anyone either.

As our communication continued, Harry constantly pursued me by asking if we could see each other. Finally, one day I agreed to start seeing him in person. He was a promoter, so he invited me to a few events that he was hosting on the east side of town, I thought it was fun and looked forward to each event. Harry loved his lifestyle. He was the life of the party; and everywhere he went, they loved him. We had a lot of fun together. After going through what I had gone through with JB, it felt good to just be free and enjoy living.

Once Harry and I decided to take our friendship to the next level, he mentioned that he wanted to ease away from the party life and focus more on elevating, but of course that never happened. Instead of leaving his party life behind, the promotion of events increased, causing him to be on the entertainment scene even more. I kind of expected that from a man who was fresh out of his divorce. Enjoying his newfound freedom was the only thing on his mind … and in some way… I understood that. Besides, from the beginning, he admitted that he wasn't ready for anything serious, and I wasn't going to rush him because neither was I.

As time passed, our friendship grew and we started to spend more time together; but I felt it was becoming a problem. So, I began to distance myself. We stayed in contact but nothing consistent. We just remained friends and I was happy with that.

The Start of the Relationship-Building Him Up From His Broken State

One year after our initial meeting, I started receiving more phone calls from Harry again. He asked if he could see me or take me out on a date. I agreed to see him. After our first date, our relationship took off - it was a great start! We did a lot of things together. During this reunion, he was driving a black SUV that I assumed was his, but later discovered that it belonged to a "lady" who he was seeing here and there. The vehicle ended up breaking down, so he eventually returned it to its owner.

After some time, Harry approached me with a question, asking if I could rent cars for him to get around until he was able to get his own vehicle. Since I had a history with the rental company and was able to get good deals on the rentals (due to my career), I didn't mind helping him out. I agreed to rent the vehicles in my name as long as he made the payments. The proposed short time of me renting cars to help him until he got on his feet turned into 6 - 8 months.

Finally, I offered to let him use my other vehicle since at the time I had two. Later, I found out that he didn't have a driver's license nor a birth certificate; but it was too late to take the car back. I cared for him so I wanted to help him as much as I could. I wanted him to be driving legally so I got all the information from him, and I ordered him about 3 copies of his birth certificate to have and to get his license back.

A few months later he went to get his license reinstated and was back driving legally again. I didn't mind doing things like this since we were a couple and that's what you do when you're in a relationship to become one and build a foundation together… or so I thought.

Sometimes, we are unaware of how the choices we make lead us to more trouble or heartache. Sometimes, we are just oblivious to how one relationship connects to another in any way. I believed I had moved on emotionally from my marriage and into a completely different relationship. I didn't recognize any similarities between my ex-husband and this new man. All I knew was that he was making me happy at the time.

In the beginning of our relationship, as I was being introduced to a lot of Harry's cousins, it seemed as though he had a huge family. Later, I found out they were just close friends that called themselves cousins since they grew up together in the same town. At this time, he shared an apartment with his "cousin" Yappo, who was welcoming and very cool. I grew to love him like a brother. Harry and I went back and forth staying overnight at each other's places. From the start, I was all in. During my stays at his place, I would cook meals for him and Yappo, clean up their apartment, wash Harry's clothes and do the dishes. At night, we enjoyed hanging out and enjoying life, having dinner at various restaurants, lounges, and bars. I really enjoyed our date nights and movie nights and so on. It was exactly what I thought dating should be.

As time went on, red flags began to appear. I probably shouldn't have ignored them, but I did. I guess I just believed that everyone has flaws and love is about accepting someone in spite of those flaws.

While I resided in Atlanta, Harry's apartment was on the East side of Atlanta. He was comfortable on that side of town and always wanted to meet up at places in Decatur and Lithonia. Since that was close to where my mother and sister lived, I didn't have a problem with it. I could visit them while I was there; but hanging out on his side of town with him soon became a blessing and a curse in a sense.

During our time together at several different places on the eastside, I received looks from women as if I wasn't supposed to be with this man. It was very annoying, but I ignored it and moved on.

One particular incident that stands out to me was one Saturday night when we went out to have some drinks and enjoy time with a few of his friends at a Smoke Lounge that one of his friends owned. There was a woman on the other side of him who kept staring at us. He was so casual and seemed unfazed by her stares; but the woman boldly came around him and taps me on my shoulder, asking if we are together. I said *"Yes, this is my boyfriend"*.

She hauled off and smacked him in the face. Then she began to punch him. He grabbed and pushed her back to restrain her from hitting him. As he was backing her out of the place, towards the door, I followed behind because I was in pure shock. She was yelling, telling me all kinds of stuff… all while continuing to punch him. She said they had been seeing each other, and that he was always going to her house in my car to come see her. She said that she had been in the car several times. Mind you, it was my vehicle I let him use since he was in need. I was thinking, *"What in the hell is going on?!"*

At this point, I was out of there. That night, I was done with him! I ignored his calls, texts, everything for about two weeks or so. Then one day, he popped up at my house making it impossible to keep ignoring him. He apologized for everything and said that he didn't want to lose me. So, I forgave him because I cared for him and wanted to believe his words. We started the relationship back up and continued to work on rebuilding.

Love can make us so forgiving. I knew that I wasn't happy with what had already transpired between us, but because I loved him… I wanted to believe that he would make things right for me… for us.

In 2016, Harry got locked up for a charge (*which will not be discussed in this book*) that was pending before we started dating. Once he found out about the warrant for his arrest, he decided to turn himself in. He called me because he needed someone to get the money and sign him out. So, he asked if I could help bail him out. We were still a couple, and I wasn't going to let him sit in jail; so, I wanted to do everything I could to help. He was still in the vehicle I loaned him, and all his belongings had been left in the car - his wallet, phone, everything.

That day, I went to the jail to pick up the vehicle to retrieve his bankcard from his wallet which was left in the car. He had provided me with his ATM code so that I could withdraw some funds from his account - something I'm sure he dreads until this day. This is not to down men or say anything that will offend them, but sometimes men are not the brightest. He made his ATM code the same as his lock code on his phone.

My next actions were not the best, but this is my story and I'm being as transparent and authentic as I can be. I had already forgiven him for the continuous cheating, and he promised things would be different; but I was curious to see if he had reverted to his old ways. So, I checked his phone and boy… why did I do that!!? I opened a can of everything I didn't want to see!! There were so many women, conversations, hookups, pictures, text messages, phone calls, anything you can think of was all in his phone. To say that I was hurt is an understatement. Once I saw what I saw and read what I read, there was no turning back. I could've ignored it and moved on like everything was okay, but it was not okay. I was not okay! I was sick of men being at the root of all my heartache. My emotions got the best of me, and I was at the point of no return. I decided to let him sit for a while.

There I was, about to help this man get out of jail and he was still playing games with me. I discovered so many messages from women he purposely introduced me to. Going through the messages in his phone made me realize that it was his way of keeping tabs on me. These women, who were actually *'his'* friends, befriended me and would update him of my whereabouts and what I was doing on a regular basis. All this information was in his phone! This normally took place at a local bar that he introduced me to, called "Dolla" where he often hung out.

While he was still in jail, my sister, a friend of mine named Jamie, and I went to a lounge called "Cigar Lounge" and saw one of the women who pretended to befriend me. I had confided in this woman, and she betrayed me. I was hurt and upset with her. Although she was his friend first, I felt disrespected. I should have known that no matter how much he did or how many games he played, her loyalty was with him and not me, but I just didn't expect her to go that low as a woman. The moment she was spotted in the lounge, we approached her to confront her. My sister and Jamie went after her, trying to drag her out of the lounge, but security stepped in. The girl ran out of the place and jumped into her car to leave. We followed her but she got away.

I felt so hurt by him and everything this woman had done. Conversations revealing that she was getting compensated by him for playing the part were in the phone as well. It showed her telling him how much her tab was, and that it was waiting for him to pay it at the bar "Dolla". I couldn't believe how deep things really were.

There were several indications in his phone where he did this quite often for her. Another incident was when this same woman tells me not to go the bar "Dolla" because it was slow. She recommended that I stay where I was, but I went to Dolla anyway. Once I got there and went inside, I saw that it was actually pretty live.

As I sat beside her, I noticed that there was another woman at the bar sitting on her other side. She never introduced me to the woman, so I found that to be weird. Especially, since I thought she was a friend. The messages in his phone affirmed the reason I was never introduced to this mystery woman. She was one of her friends but was also someone Harry was seeing behind my back. Just when I was starting to think things couldn't get any worse.

Once again that was in his phone when I went through it while he was locked up. It showed play by play. How I was at the bar with his side piece, and she was in between us, keeping us from talking to each other. *Like really? What kind of woman does that? Women can be so messy!* Then to top it all off, she left her tab at the bar for him to come back later and pay for it. This was the logistics of their friendship… if things went well in his favor, he covered her tab.

So, judge me or judge me not after that… all bets were off. It was on site at that point when we saw her. That's the reason when I saw her at the Smoke Lounge, my friends reacted the way they did. I'm glad I have grown out of that mentality. It took some soul searching and prayers to get to where I am today! Still, the hurt of those revelations is unforgettable. I've been through some things that I'm not proud of, but hey… haven't we all?

Giving Him What He Wanted

After my discovery of this betrayal, I wanted to just leave the relationship and end everything dealing with Harry. I was done with the disrespect and his refusal to change his ways. I told him since he wasn't ready for a relationship, he could continue to do what he was doing and be single. To be honest, I knew better. I knew I shouldn't have invested so much of my emotions into being with him because from the start Harry warned me that he wasn't looking for anything serious. I guess I wanted him to be the man, I thought he could be and that hope kept me from seeing him for the man he truly was. It hurt more than anything because I ignored every sign and all the red flags which meant I was the real cause of my own heartache.

The day Harry turned himself in was close to the weekend because he didn't want to miss too many days of work. Unfortunately, he was unable to get out of jail right away and had to do a few days behind bars until he saw a judge on the following Monday. Since I agreed to help him before I found out about all the betrayal, I stuck to my word. I handled everything Harry needed me to. I even contacted his supervisor to ensure that he didn't lose his job. For him to get out of jail, he needed to show proof that he did community service and a letter from his former probation officer saying this was completed. At first, I had no idea where to start but then I decided to start with finding out who his former probation officer was and go from there. I made a few calls and did all the leg work, with the help of a friend. Harry also needed proof of the hours completed, classes he was supposed to take and proof of any payments, which I paid.

On the day that Harry went before the judge, he didn't have all the required documents, so the case had to be delayed. A week later was his next hearing and Harry asked me to speak on his behalf since he had no one to do so. I spoke to the judge on Harry's character and how being imprisoned could affect his job since he had been there so long. Afterwards, we were informed that once bail was paid, he could be released that day if all the required documents were submitted, which I provided the courts proof of. During the process, I continued to stay in contact with his boss to make sure she was updated and aware of his release. I kept my word and helped Harry get out of jail.

Through all of that, I still carried the pain of his betrayal and disrespect. Knowing everything and still helping him through it all was a heavy load to carry. I had no time to process it all while he was in jail since my only focus was on helping him get released. After he got out, we went back to my house since that's where my car that he was driving was. He thanked me for helping him and was very apologetic and that was that. I told him that I needed time, and I asked him to leave.

Life went on and Harry went back to work. He was still hanging out and doing what he was doing before he went in. For a while, I didn't call or text him, but he would constantly call and blow my phone up – still trying to apologize. One day he visited my home with flowers and gifts, claiming that things were about to change, and he needed me by his side. He said he appreciated me for being there during some hard times for him. He admitted that he was guarded, and it took him a while to fully trust people. Then he opened up about his childhood and what he experienced when he lost his mother so that I would sympathize with his situation.

He had confided in me about what happened to his mother when he was a teenager. He was broken and hurt. As we sat in the living room, he shared that after his mother passed, he moved away to Philly with his aunt and uncle who raised him. He also shared that because he moved away, his siblings felt as if he had left them behind so his relationship with them was strained. At this point, I got to know a little more about him than I already knew. A part of me wanted to help him through what he went through instead of turning my back on him. I didn't want to be yet another person to let him down. I should've known that I couldn't help anyone through childhood trauma. That was out of my knowledge and skills. I didn't grow up the same way as he did, so I didn't know where to start. I just thought if I poured into him and gave him as much love as I could, he would change and be better. As time passed it didn't seem to be enough. I felt sorry for him quite naturally, it was easy for me being a woman having that compassion, as I always had. I wanted to be there for him and help him through the voids and past traumas, but he needed more. This is where he should've started therapy and where I should have stepped back to let him deal (or not deal) with this alone. I just couldn't get myself to do it.

----- Forwarded Message -----
From: "Dianca Wiley" <██████@yahoo.com>
To: "jpurys@co.henry.ga.us" <jpurys@co.henry.ga.us>

˅ Hide original message

Sent: Thu, Nov 5, 2020 at 11:34 AM
Subject: Fw: Harry Lamont Sanders court date

Hello Joela,

I have attached the letter Harry received from his doctor on today. He does need to have another surgery procedure due to some complications and I'm not sure as of now when it will be. Here is the letter that you need to show he is actively battling and fighting to get through this cancer process.

Let me know if you need anything else on our end.

Thanks again for help with this
Dianca

Taking The Relationship
To The
Next Level

The Beginning Of Life As Becoming An Adult

In 2016, topics such as, how much money we would save if we just moved in together began to surface. This is when Harry and I decided to take the next step in the relationship. Even though I wasn't too sure about it when those talks came up, Harry was very persuasive. Eventually, I was open to the idea. Besides, it was almost like we already lived together because most of the time he was at my house. I began to think, *why not move in together?* In addition, my house was only 15 minutes away from his job, and he loved the shorter commute.

When this talk of us living together came up, I actually considered selling or renting the house out, but Harry was very persistent on just keeping the house and staying there. We built a lot together in the home. We painted it, inside and out, and redid some light fixtures and changed out my downstairs bathroom. All my major upgrades were done in June 2020 during covid, regardless of what you were told or heard. I upgraded my home during that time due to wanting to change it and remodel some things about it. There has been a story painted of me so

I am going to go into detail about everything that happened so everyone will have a clear understanding of the facts.

Harry and I were in a relationship, so I helped him with several things that needed to be done as well. He knew a lot of people so instead of me paying a random person he would call his friends over to fix things. We shared the expenses of the home repairs.

He and I had some great times together as we did a lot of traveling. From weddings and family events located out of state, to the trips we took together and the ones where we included all our kids. My love for his children is sincere and real. I won't mention too much about the children, out of respect for them; but I will forever love and do for them as long as needed. When Harry and I were together, I loved them like my own and still do. Towards the end of the relationship, the connection I had with his daughter became a little rocky, but we talked and got through the issues we were having. Thankfully, we were able to come together during a tough time of her father's sickness. We laughed and shed a lot of tears together. During that time, our bond became more special. On the weekends, when they visited, I would wake up on Sunday morning and take them to church with me and my children. While I attended the regular worship service, they would go to the children's church. Harry never wanted to go; so, he would stay at home. I never let his decisions waiver my faith. *2 Corinthians 6:14* - *Be ye not unequally yoked together with unbelievers: for what fellowship hath righteousness with unrighteousness?*

My relationship with Harry was alright but wasn't perfect at that point. I didn't go back through his phone, but I felt that he was still up to something. We continued to hang out and he kept bringing me around all his friends. Most of them knew what he was up to, but of course no one said anything to me. They just kept quiet and stayed out of it. Everyone knew what was going on was wrong, but no one had the nerve to say anything to him about his behavior. I get it - it wasn't their place to say anything; but if you see someone you call a friend messing up and playing around, then that is your business. I felt too many people were going with the flow rather than being true and telling him he was wrong for some of his actions.

I know this as facts because I used to ask him, "Did any of his friends know what you were doing?" Later, he admitted and told me who all knew of what he was doing. I won't mention the names because they know who they are. Harry did mention, on several occasions, that his brother Larry called him out on his choices and behaviors, but he didn't listen. In the end, it was up to Harry to make the changes. It just baffles me how many people were close to him, loved him, hung out with him, talked to him and just were his friend but didn't call him out or address what he was doing? I can't say that I would have left him had they told me but I can say that I wish someone had said something. They all played a role in my pain because no one did. The cycle of hurt with him only kept going and eventually got worse.

Regardless of what he was faced with, he didn't have the right to continue living how he was living. I can't expect people to have a conscious on things that had nothing to do with them, but I did expect them to have compassion for what I was being put through as a result. I decided to stop worrying about it and do my own thing at that point. I heard things from some of his people, siblings, and his drinking buddies and some of mine as well. I would get pictures of him out and they would tell me what he was up to; most of my information came from anonymous numbers. I tried to ignore it because I loved him and wasn't ready for the relationship to end, but it was hard. Especially, when what he was telling me didn't add up with what I was being told. Despite the anonymous warnings and even my own intuition that something was off, I continued to ignore everything- all of which ended up being the truth in the end.

In 2019 is when I found out about this "lady" he was seeing, I really had no solid proof. There were just whispers of his lies and secret hookups with her around the local bar "Dolla" in which he went to quite often after work. *Here we go again*, was all I could think and feel.

I Decided To Get Even

After a few months of feeling uncomfortable in this relationship and having a feeling he wasn't being faithful in May of 2019, I decided to get even and cheat back with a guy I had met. Now, I'm not glorifying my choice or what I did but it happened. Looking back, I wished I would've had enough strength to just walk away from it all. I was so hurt that I wanted him to feel the same pain. From the beginning, the guy I met knew I was seeing someone and was in a relationship, so that wasn't a secret to him. I was up front and honest from the start. I saw him for a few months and then at the end of the year both of our intuitions finally came and slapped us both in our faces. 12/31/2019 is when Harry found out I was seeing someone else.

Let me put all the rumors to bed and tell you the facts versus the "Bar Chatter". I was out with the guy I was seeing and we went to a liquor store to grab some drinks. I was going to have a few drinks with him before I went home to bring in the new year. Well, while we were there, Harry pulled up to the same liquor store in the area he normally hung out at, close by "Dolla". Okay, let me admit that I was sloppy on purpose. I had checked out of the relationship long before that night because I knew he was cheating but never had concrete proof. I no longer cared if he knew since he didn't really care how he hurt me with what he had been doing for years. He approached the car as the guy was coming out the store. He knocked on the window. I looked at him and told him we could talk later. He kept knocking on the window and demanded that we talk right then. I told him that it wasn't the time. The guy was puzzled but eventually got into the car. I was driving my sister's car that night because Harry had my car. My Lexus that he normally drove was in the shop. I left the store and was going to take the guy back to his house since I had only picked him up to go grab some drinks, since it was easier since I had his car blocked in. The guy was upset. Harry was upset. I was over that night at that point.

As we were riding toward his house, I looked in my rear-view mirror and I saw Harry following us. I passed the guys house on purpose so he wouldn't know where the guy lived and cause more drama. Well, he followed and didn't stop following us. It was a hot mess for sure. Finally, I got tired of him following us, so I dropped him off and I headed home.

I couldn't believe that he was acting as if he had been doing everything right and being a faithful man who had discovered my infidelity. Why did he take me through all of that like he barely cared about me… then when I did the same, he wanted to get to the bottom of things? That was not the time for us to talk or handle our issues, but I get it, what's good for the goose is good for the gander. Women just can't do the same things our men do to us.

I left and was very upset with the way he tried to approach and resolve things in that moment. Yes, he had every right to… two wrongs don't make it right; but at that time, I could care less. I was over it and really still hurt by what he had been doing. Later, I found out he stopped and talked to the guy about us. Harry claims the guy was telling him everything and doing most of the talking. The guy later said Harry was the one asking questions and doing most of the talking. I honestly didn't care which was true. I was over it and done with the situation on both sides. I was upset and I know he was upset. I knew I hurt him, and I did feel bad, but I was more hurt by all that I had accepted and put up with from him. So, I wanted him to feel what I felt.

I went back home at that point; the night was over with. He later followed me and of course we started arguing about it. By the end of the conversation, I was in tears because I knew I hurt him. At that moment, I was not thinking about all the hurt he had caused me in the past. I just focused on what I did to him. I kept apologizing and telling him I was sorry for how I hurt him and how I handled things. He left very upset and immediately went to the local bar "Dolla". He spent New Years Eve with this lady friend. I found out later that night when he came back home very late from partying that night. Perfect opportunity I thought, so I went through his phone. *Yeah-yeah, I know, if you go looking for something you will find it!* Find "it" I did!

I mean I already knew, but that night, I needed to see it. After what I saw, I knew then that the relationship was over. He had been seeing this lady for some time at least from 2018 from what I could prove with what I saw in his phone. She also put things out confirming this!

From what I was told, her family member from the bar "Dolla" introduced them and she didn't agree with the relationship at first, but things went how they went. It happened and it was what it was. In his phone, I found all kinds of pictures of them at different events, bars, her home, and of course a whole thread of text messages. I had all the proof I needed. I told him that I was done.

Instead of him owning up to what he had been doing for years, he made me feel horrible about what I had done to him just that one time. Keep in mind, that he was doing it and doing it much longer and out in the open. Once again, I'm not excusing my actions but damn! How much more could I have taken at this point. He said he wanted to make it work and cried and begged for me not to give up on him. I said it was over and I wanted him out. I was so determined to stand my ground this time. My feelings had to be more important than he was to me.

A few days after this, he showed the kids a ring and said he wanted to marry me. Really, perfect opportunity. Now that I finally wanted it to be over, he wanted to pull out the ring. I loved him dearly, but I wasn't putting up with his behavior a day longer. I had to show him I was serious and not just talking!

Harry Moved Out

After that, things were very awkward. Harry and I grew distant as the days and weeks went on. We rarely talked and when we did, he just expressed that he wanted things to work between us. I didn't see it working without a change occurring. How could I possibly keep forgiving him and we still be able to trust one another? As much as I wanted our relationship to work, I just didn't see it happening at that point. I hated to end things, but I couldn't keep accepting the disrespect from him. Neither one of our actions were right but forgiving him would only put me right back where I didn't want to be… in position to get played again. I knew we had to make a change and it started with our living situation. He had to leave if there was even a slight chance of whatever we still had working at all in our future. We needed distance to see if this was what either of us really wanted. January of 2020 he moved out. He said he didn't want to end things but, in my mind, I knew we needed a break from the toxic situation we had going on. He claimed to be moving in with a former neighbor of his, an older man who owned his own home and had plenty of room for him. I rolled with his story even though I didn't fully believe it. No longer could I allow myself to worry about what he was doing.

From the start, I knew we shouldn't have moved in together. He wasn't even fully truthful with himself and I knew that, but once again I ignored the red flags. I was trying to see the good in the situation. I wanted to see what it could be rather than what it truly was. He wanted to still work on the relationship and see if we can do it living separately, but I kept telling him I was done. I kept trying to make it clear and I never led him on. I truly was done!

About a month after Harry moved out, I went to a local sports bar on the other side of town from where we normally hung out to watch the game. I was with the same guy he saw me with late last year. The guy and I had gotten a little bit closer due to the circumstances. We decided to try a new place out, so I thought it would be cool. This was a totally different bar from the one Harry normally hung out at but the same general area. I didn't think I would run into him or anyone for that matter since it was a new spot, boy was I wrong!

Harry told me that he had moved in with a former neighbor, but the truth was he moved in with that lady (at that time, I didn't know - but it'll make sense later). We sat down at a table upstairs with my sister and a friend, Jamie. It was them that noticed Harry was there. I was immediately thinking in my head, *goodness I don't want any trouble*. I wanted to go but the guy I was with was saying he wanted us to stay and that it would be fine. He seemed cool like there would be no issues. I should've known better, but I stayed.

The whole night, Harry was giving me looks that let me know he was not happy at all about seeing me there – especially, with another man. I was upstairs watching the game on the big screen and Harry was looking up at me from the bar downstairs where he was sitting.

After a few drinks, I headed downstairs to the restroom and as I was leaving the restroom and heading back to my table up the stairs, Harry came and asked if we could talk. I told him not then or there. I suggested that maybe later we could discuss things, hoping that would be okay and he would walk off. He didn't like that I didn't stop to talk about things and got upset. We stood on the stairs for about two minutes talking and going back and forth about why I didn't stop at that moment to talk to him. Finally, I told him I would talk to him later and proceeded to walk off. That upset him even more. I'm not sure what he was feeling but it was probably embarrassment and hurt. Especially since a few people from the local bar "Dolla" were there as well. I didn't notice until later. He shoved me down while holding his beer and it wasted all over me. I fell to the ground and was wet from his beer. I was in pure shock, he had never allowed his anger to escalate to anything physical. We have never taken it to the point where he put his hands on me. I wasn't hurt in any way from the shove but just in shock it happened at all. My sister was almost to the top of the stairs and immediately saw what happened. She yelled for the guy who was upstairs still sitting down. The guy stormed down and tried to swing on Harry but they both fell to the ground; and it was broken up by security. There was no fight, just both of them falling to the ground and tussling. I got up in attempt to run over to them to break it up, but people were holding me back. The bar employees called the police, and they had three witnesses who confirmed what had happened and gave statements. I didn't want the police involved at all. Later that night, Harry called me and asked to talk. He said that he was not worried about any of that - he still just wanted to talk to me.

I told him that the police were called, and they were looking for him to get his side of the story. He didn't care and only cared about talking to me. I was hurt that it had to get to that point. We never had to involve the police in anything before, during the entire relationship. A warrant was issued for him the next morning. Eventually, he turned himself in and from jail, he called me once again to help him out.

I felt bad for him and I felt like I was the reason he was there. So, I agreed to help. I know some may wonder, why did I agree to help him out, especially since I was over it and done. He was no longer my concern or responsibility; but the truth is, I still loved and cared for him regardless of how he treated me over the years. So, that's why.

At this time, which was 2020, I did not know that he was living with another woman. The case is left open during covid but not acted on until 2021. I called the prosecutor who reached out to me about the case in 2021 and I asked them if they could close the case due to all he was facing with his health (which will be discussed later in this book). I told them I would not be cooperating with the case if they decided to move forward. The prosecuting attorney asked for proof that he was dealing with health issues. I provided her a letter directly from the doctor that was treating him for his health problems. The first letter I got via email was dated 11/2020. They requested another letter, this time one that was detailed with his diagnosis, so I got the second letter 12/2020.

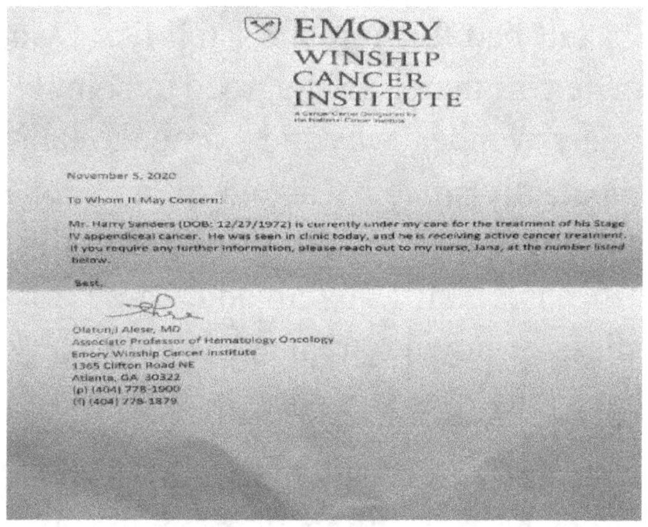

EMORY
WINSHIP
CANCER
INSTITUTE
A Cancer Center Designated by
the National Cancer Institute

November 5, 2020

To Whom It May Concern:

Mr. Harry Sanders (DOB: 12/27/1972) is currently under my care for the treatment of his Stage IV appendiceal cancer. He was seen in clinic today, and he is receiving active cancer treatment. If you require any further information, please reach out to my nurse, Jana, at the number listed below.

Best,

Olatunji Alese, MD
Associate Professor of Hematology Oncology
Emory Winship Cancer Institute
1365 Clifton Road NE
Atlanta, GA 30322
(p) (404) 778-1900
(f) (404) 778-1879

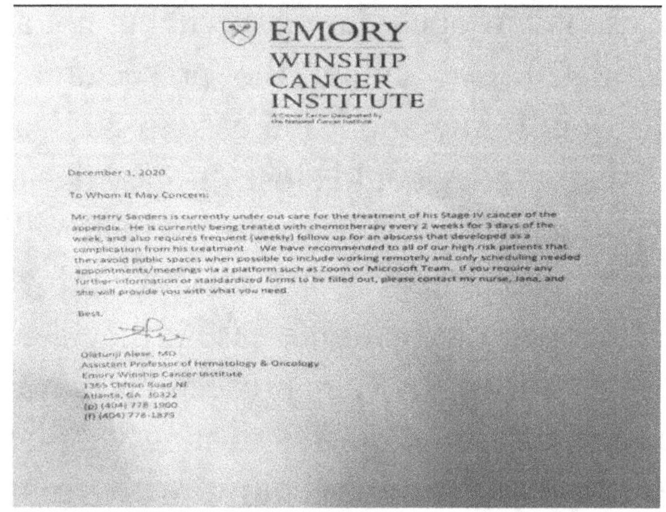

EMORY
WINSHIP
CANCER
INSTITUTE
A Cancer Center Designated by
the National Cancer Institute

December 1, 2020

To Whom It May Concern:

Mr. Harry Sanders is currently under out care for the treatment of his Stage IV cancer of the appendix. He is currently being treated with chemotherapy every 2 weeks for 3 days of the week, and also requires frequent (weekly) follow up for an abscess that developed as a complication from his treatment. We have recommended to all of our high risk patients that they avoid public spaces when possible to include working remotely and only scheduling needed appointments/meetings via a platform such as Zoom or Microsoft Team. If you require any further information or standardized forms to be filled out, please contact my nurse, Jana, and she will provide you with what you need.

Best,

Olatunji Alese, MD
Assistant Professor of Hematology & Oncology
Emory Winship Cancer Institute
1365 Clifton Road NE
Atlanta, GA 30322
(p) (404) 778-1900
(f) (404) 778-1879

CHAPTER 5

Therapy Is Needed Counseling
4/2020 – 7/2020

*a*fter the bar incident happened, Harry wanted to make things work even more. He suggested that we go to couple's therapy. At first, I was hesitant but later I agreed to attend with him because he said he didn't want to lose me. I told him if he wanted it to work, he needed to make changes because he wanted to and not just because I left him. He paid for therapy and agreed to work it out. For three months, we attended pre-marital counseling. We saw a couple who was married and specialized in premarital therapy as well; but it ended as quick as it began. During the sessions, Harry wasn't engaged. He said just enough to get by but didn't put actions behind his words… neither did he do any of the homework assignments. It became obvious to me that it had been just a ploy to get me back.

One day, the therapists called me and said they didn't want to keep taking Harry's money, especially since he wasn't showing any progress. They said that it was clear he was just wasting time. So, they said they were ending the sessions until Harry became honest with himself. Mind you, couple's therapy was not my idea… it was

Harry's. He offered to do it and paid the cost- just to go and not take it seriously. Honestly, I was fine with how things were at that time since we were no longer living together. I didn't have to deal with the lies, hurt, and disrespect anymore. It's really crazy how far a person can be willing to go just to play with you.

A few months after our therapy sessions ended, the therapists reached out to me to ask how things were. I informed them that no changes had been made. They advised me to let it go with him and move on. They said Harry was not changing, and I could not change him. He had to want to change for himself. I should've taken their advice then, but I didn't. I stayed around a little while longer.

One particular moment after therapy, I recall him talking about his divorce and why it was so hard for him to trust anyone or open his heart. He had never done this before and that was the issue. We should've talked about our past and what we had been through because it was major to where we were mentally at the time. I did, but it was hard for him to. He made it seem like it was all her fault and I just listened to him vent about what had happened. I had no reason to doubt what he was sharing. I was only going by what he told me. I should've known there was way more to his story. Later, after speaking with family close to him, I got the whole truth about a portion of why his marriage ended. He basically did to his ex the same things he was doing to me.

Side note: Harry's ex-wife and I have had no issues whatsoever. We actually had a great relationship. She is very educated, sophisticated, well put together and all about her business. I admired and still do admire her strength to this day!

Harry Starts Calling
My Family and Friends

Harry began to call, text, and meet up with my family and friends to try and save the relationship. I understood that he wasn't over it but I wasn't impressed. I felt like the same energy he put into reaching out to them could've been the same energy he put into working on himself and becoming a better man. Those changes never came! One of my friends, Lisa, was very spiritual and always listened to him when he called or reached out. I think he felt more connected with her because he never really had the spiritual portion in his life. I never saw him pray other than the prayers I led with him. I believe he felt led to connect with her more on that level since she was always there to pray and listen to his issues or concerns. Lisa saw something in him as well, and she said it seemed genuine after talking with him. She is the same friend that was there when I first met Harry, so it was special for her.

After speaking with Lisa and having her reveal to me that he had been reaching out to her on multiple occasions - in hopes of saving the relationship, he showed her a ring. He said he wanted to propose but he was hurting and wanted to make sure that I was all in. *How could I possibly be all in when he lived with another woman? NO way!* Once again, this wasn't brought to my attention until December of 2020. Prior to that, I still believed that he lived with the older guy from his old place.

Lisa talked with him over several months letting him know he couldn't have this lady and me too. She told him that he couldn't expect me to not move on unless he showed me more than just talking about it. He insisted it was nothing between him and the other lady and he was waiting on me to see if I was serious. Lisa made it seem like he was very sincere, he would even shed tears with her. So… yet again, I decided to keep seeing him to see for myself if he was serious this time. He went even further to convince me this time by starting his own one on one sessions with a therapist after the couples therapy ended. I felt like that was my sign to keep going and not give up; I had finally seen change!

Side note - You should never make moves based on potential behaviors versus shown behaviors. This is something I struggled with. I'm a cancer so I see the good in people. I try to focus on what they could be and how they could act versus what I've already been shown. *In reality, potential is not a realistic possibility of who and what they could be but our own mind telling us what we would do if in that same situation.*

Focusing On My Home

Covid was in full swing and the world had shut down. Since I was working from home and was always there, I decided to give my focus to other things that mattered at that time. It was time to get my house in order. Finally, I could handle all the new upgrades both inside and outside of the home I wanted to make. I had contractors always in and out, getting quotes and starting new projects. I started with the backsplash in my entire kitchen and bar area. I had the carpet ripped up and changed it to laminate tile flooring all downstairs. I added ceiling fans in a few rooms, changed out door frames to my home, changed windows and window panels on the outside, extended my deck to be bigger, cut down all trees and had a huge retainer wall built from one end of the home to the other end. I also planted 20 rose bushes on the hill and got sod installed in the front back and all around my home. All this work was started in June 2020 and ended about July 2021. The person responsible for the flooring was actually referred to me by Harry. He would come over and stay during the time of several installs. A few of the installs would be after a few of his appointments and he would talk with his friend while his workers worked on the floors. During this time of improving my home, Harry would come by very often and see the changes. He would come and lay down and take naps in between his visits. He told me he wanted to come back there several times. It went in one ear and out the other, they were just more broken promises in my eyes. I was changing my home to provide a new life for my children and I, and possibly extra income once we moved into another home. I was planning on moving forward.

Broken Promises
vs
Health Battles & Diagnoses

Harry gave deadline after deadline on when he wanted to move back in. He even brought back several of his clothing, shoes, and jewelry, to make me believe he was wanting to save the relationship. All along, he was just not wanting to let go of everything he had with me… even with whatever else he had going on. I tried to move on, but he would not let it go. He would pop up late at nights, early mornings, and several times throughout the day. He said it was to see me but I knew it was to make sure I never felt comfortable having another man in that space.

In July 2020, we took a trip to Florida for my birthday with my daughter, my best friend (Maggie), and her girls. We had a great time just being a family, but we were taking things slow.

Throughout the trip, he kept complaining of cramps at times. He used to talk about cramping in the past, when we did live together, but he always dismissed it as gas. I tried to take charge and make appointments for him in the past but since he worked in a hospital, he said he would handle it. He had his personal doctor at his job, so I let him handle it. After each supposed doctor's visit, he would tell me, it's just gas and he just had to watch what he eats. He would take some tums to relieve the gas and cramps. It would go away and wouldn't come back for months at a time. I had no reason to doubt him since he worked in the hospital setting. I cared about him, but I couldn't watch everything he did. I was raising two kids; so, he would just have to take care of himself like any reasonable adult would. With one kid getting ready to head off to college and the other one in middle school at the time, I just didn't have it in me to press the issue any further. Little did I know, he hadn't gone to any of the doctor's appointments and wasn't checking up on his health like he used to tell me he was. When we got back from our trip, he told me he was going to the ER due to the cramps getting worse. Shortly after that, they diagnosed him with cancer. This was horrible for me to find out and I tried my best to keep it together. It was so hard seeing a man who I had been in a relationship with and stood by his side to get so sick so suddenly. That hurt but I had to just be real with myself and keep my life going for me and my children since he was where he was. I did remain close to him. I don't know a man alive that wouldn't want someone by his side to help him through a battle like the one he faced. I expressed this to him and that's when I started to realize he wasn't living where he told me he was, but once again I had no proof of this just only my intuition. Things were just off.

He had his surgery that year, to try to remove the cancer shortly after we got back from Florida. I fully expected him to try and get me to spend more time with him at his place but that was not the case. That's when I had to take a step back and question what he was telling me. Once again, I still didn't know he lived with anyone other than an older neighbor from his former neighborhood. I just couldn't shake the feeling he wasn't telling the whole truth. I just watched and kept my eyes open to everything.

Therapy Is Needed

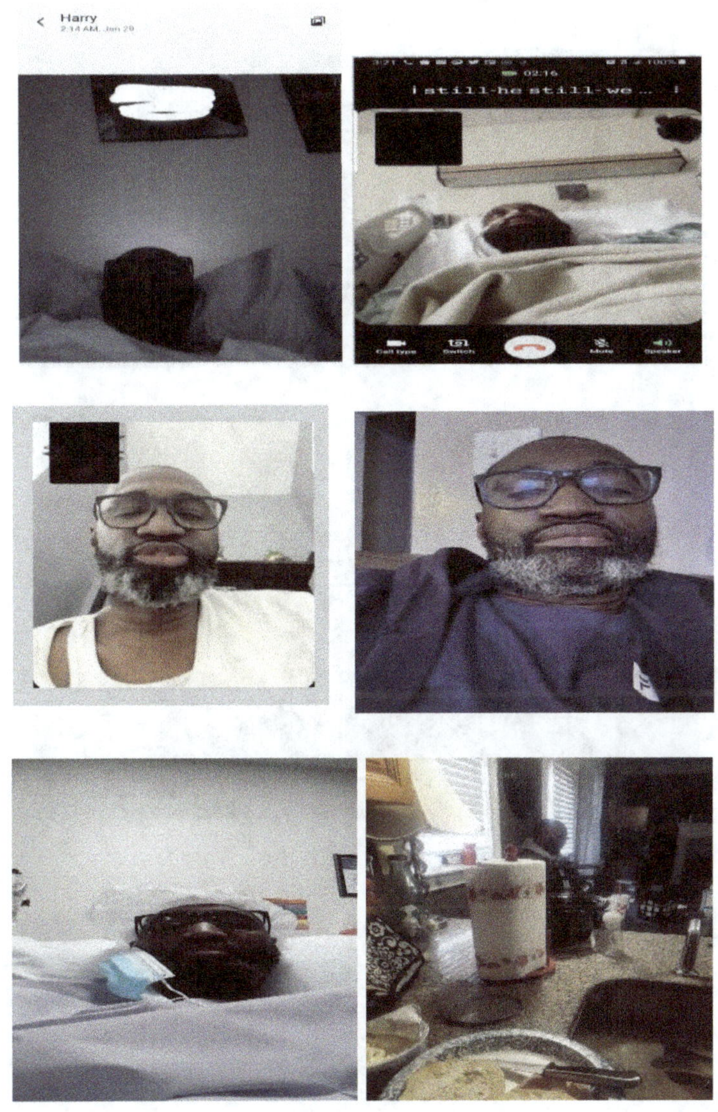

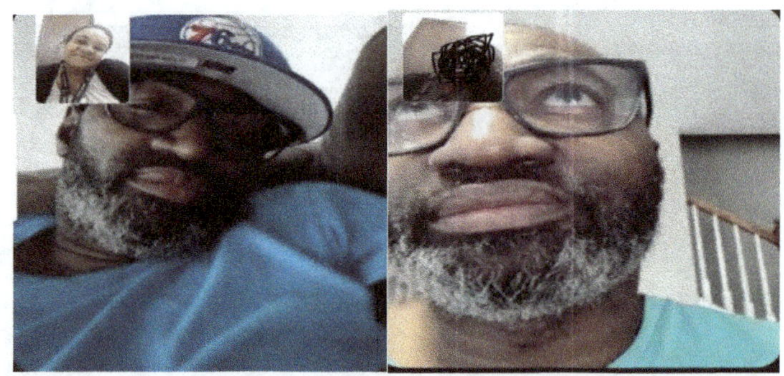

The Truth Finally Revealed

I finally got the proof and confirmation that I needed. Harry had not been honest with me about his living situation. In December of 2020, I found out he was living with this lady for good and not the lies he continued to tell me. I made this discovery by reaching out to her because I got tired of the excuses and lies. I was upset when I reached out to her. No, I'm not blaming her because he knew what he was doing. but she knew he was in a relationship as well. You will see later in the book the proof that she knew he had someone – Hell, everyone knew that. It didn't stop either of them. She never tried to reach out to me or ask me anything. So, it seemed like she was just content to let things be whatever it was. All I wanted was for him to be real and honest about things. He was still doing whatever best suited him. Letting me go live my life and move on just didn't suit his ego. Instead of saying this and confessing to his shortcomings, he said everything he could to convince me that I was wrong about him.

I wanted to believe him even though I felt he was lying yet again. He had an excuse for everything, and he always seem to twist things in his favor, but this was something he couldn't twist. After contacting this lady, she said he moved in with her and had been there since February 2020; she showed proof of this as well.

A few days later, Sherri, a friend of mine, saw him out on his birthday (December 27, 2020) with this lady. She asked Harry if he lived there with the lady, he said he didn't. Later that night, she saw the lady and asked her if he lived with her. She said he did. This same night, he was at my house apologizing from 2:30 am until 5am. He was fussing on the phone with my best friend Lisa, whom he called while he was in my bedroom, and explaining to her why he lied to me after I asked him to just leave me alone and let me be happy. After that I was completely done with him… or so I thought.

He refused to leave me alone. It's crazy because this is the same year that he had his first surgery. He kept drinking and smoking hookahs after being advised to stop! People will do what they want to do! Later, he had no choice but to admit it, but he was still lying saying he moved in with her in June 2020 and only because she asked him to (his words).

It's so ironic how love can feel so good and so bad. It can make you feel so high even as that person you're so in love with tears you down. It can take you for such a loop that you can't tell up from down. I was so in love, that's why even when I knew he was lying, I still wanted to believe him. Why even when I told myself I was done with this man, I would find myself right back by his side.

CHAPTER 6

They Say, Hurt People Hurt People

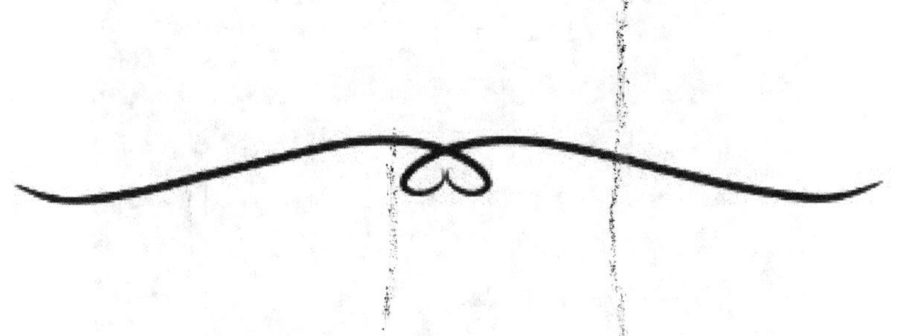

Lost Loved Ones

*I*n August 2020, one of Harry's aunts that raised him in Philly passed away and he was torn up about it. Then in October of 2020, he showed up to my house about 2 or 3 am, let himself in, and I woke up after feeling someone sit on the end of the bed. He started crying and told me he lost his brother Johnny who was a twin. Johnny was in a horrible car accident. I felt so bad for him experiencing so many tragedies in his life, up until that point. He told me he was leaving to head to the hospital to view the body. I was trying to be there for him as much as I could but how could I when he constantly fed me little by little- just enough to keep me in his life.

February 24, 2021, he lost his longtime friend and our family attorney who did work for us both, in a deadly car crash. Just one death after another it seems.

Then came February 25, 2021, he lost his father, due to health battles and contracting covid. He felt bad about this being that he had so many unanswered questions for his father. He had been holding that pain in but there was so much he wanted to talk to his father about.

A moment that stuck out to me is when he told me while he was visiting his father in a South Carolina hospital, he asked him, "Is there anything you want to tell me", hoping his dad would open up to him about his mother's passing. He said his dad said no. He said his dad didn't open up to him like he wanted him to regarding things that happened in the past. Harry was still holding on to all of the pain and other emotions of not knowing what really happened. There was a lot of childhood trauma that he was dealing with that he never got through. I won't mention the details of his mother's passing, but it was truly hurtful to hear of how he lost his mother at such a young age. This was horrible, so many people lost their lives in a short time and each time he seemed to be losing another piece of himself.

This tore him up and he was supposed to be focused on himself and what he was dealing with, but he had so many people around him leaving this world. I understood, and I took more time to myself and let him mourn all those losses. I really wanted him to focus on himself and healing his body, but healing his body was taking a backseat to the healing of his heart and soul. This seemed to be waking him up and opening his eyes to reality though. He still came around, called, and reached out to me daily during this time, so, I stayed by his side.

F*ck cancer

One month after we came back from my birthday trip in July 2020, Harry was diagnosed with Stage four Appendix cancer. I had access to all his logins, so I logged in often to see if the doctor's visit and bills lined up with what he was saying because he was so guarded on what he told anyone. He didn't want anyone feeling sorry for him. He didn't even reveal to his close family and best friends he had cancer right away; it came months later. I remained in contact with him because I was concerned about his health and didn't want to see him in pain or facing health challenges. I stayed by his side until the end. I had to finally move on and not be in that sad space anymore; but I never cut off communication with him. I was the friend he didn't know to allow himself to need.

His 1st surgery was September 2020. His 2nd surgery was June 2022. They were unable to get all the cancer out due to it being attached to a major artery. He went to several chemo sessions, then became too weak to do any more sessions. I was watching a man I had once loved more than even I understood deteriorate right before my eyes and it was devastating.

On one particular day when he came over, he seemed to have something heavy on his mind. He said that he wanted to talk. I cooked him breakfast and we talked about several different things. This day, he wanted to apologize yet again for everything that had happened between us. I tried to stop him because at this point, I no longer cared about the apologies. I knew he was sorry, but his health was all I was focused on. Still, I knew he was being sincere about everything and was very genuine about what he was saying. He broke down and started to cry and told me how he felt like he was being punished for how he treated me and other women in his past. He said he felt this was his karma and if it was, he was willing to accept it. If this was what his journey was supposed to be… he accepted it. I immediately hugged him and told him that no matter how he felt, he was chosen to go through this for a reason. I told him God makes no mistakes and he needed to get closer to God to repent for everything he felt he had done wrong. I also reminded him no one is perfect, and we all go through battles. I said to him, "You will be set free from everything once you have your time with God."

Harry was very strong for getting as far as he had gotten, with such a tough battle. I don't even know if I could've endured what he had gone through with his health up to that point; in that moment, I knew that whatever happens God would get him through it.

He began to cry again. I just listened, laid there, and tried to comfort him as best as I could. He went to sleep from there. That was our moment, and it was a great moment that I'll forever be grateful for. I never had hate in my heart for him at all. I hated his ways and the decisions he made but who was I to judge him? I wasn't his Maker. He had a higher God to answer to on that and I believe he spoke to God and was forgiven for everything he prayed for!

Another Sit Down With Lisa

One day Harry and I sat down with my best friend, Lisa, and she asked him, "Why do you keep reaching out to me about my friend? You say you want her back, but your actions are not matching your words. Wassup?"

He really was just speechless and didn't want to say anything since he knew the truth was out and he didn't know how to handle it. Then the question came out while I stepped away from the table, she asked, "What is holding you there?... What kind of nurse is she?"

His silence broke as he said, "Oncologist!"

When I returned, they both gave me the news. Lisa said, "Shana, I get it now". She asked, "Do you know what type of nurse she is?" I said "No, how would I know that?"

Then Lisa told me. I started to get it at that moment. Lisa grabbed my hand and grabbed his and asked how I felt about it. I said I was hurt due to everything he put me through and not being honest from the start, all while still asking me to wait for him. I let him know that I understood and I will never ask him to forget about his health to make things work for us. I just wanted him to live his life and stop holding me from moving on, since he made the choice to be where he was. I told him if she would help get him better and it would be easier for him during that time, then please stay there! All of us started crying as we held hands. It was a special moment not many people even know or will understand.

It was a moment of true understanding but at that moment, I had to change my way of thinking about all of it. I focused on his health and not my feelings toward the situation I was already a part of. Many will not understand why I stuck by him, well here is the answer. I wanted to, and I felt led to. God told me not to leave his side at that time and I didn't. I knew the relationship was done because mentally, I couldn't keep doing what he wanted me to for his own personal gain. I'm human, I have feelings and a life too and I had to move on with it!

Care Packages/Back and Forth

Harry used to come to my house all the time and we would go to Emory to pick up care packages for him. They contained all kinds of fruits vegetables, healthy snacks, water, juices etc. His boss and another coworker would call or text me telling me when to go get them. He would come to the house, and I would drive him to the hospital to pick them up and greet several different coworkers.

After one of his surgeries, a lot of coworkers came out to greet him and were overjoyed and happy to see him. It was a very special moment for him. They even gave him cards filled with money and sweet words of encouragement. He had a lot of support and I'm glad he did. It may have seemed like I was the crazy ex, that some had painted me out to be, but I was far from that! I wasn't highlighted as a support system at all and that is alright; but I was very much supportive to him all the way through this process and right up to the end. I provided him emotional, physical, and mental support all the way through this process. He wasn't married to either of us, so I stood by him since he asked me to be there and I wasn't going anywhere while he battled this illness!

EMORY
HEALTHCARE
Food &
Nutrition
2016

The Betrayal of
My Family and I Being Discussed

During January 2021, after finding out he lived there. I got a hold of some messages discussing my family and I, my home and other things about me and Harry's relationship. It hurt for sure at first but then it turned into disgust. I was disgusted finding out how an adult could speak in a manner about me to a child, then try to turn the child against me! Very sad!

Regardless of what you were told about me and how I was portrayed to be the crazy ex, being an adult, you should have been bigger and not fixed your mouth to discuss me. Especially, to a child. Later you would find out all you were told were lies and I was far from the "crazy ex". I will not put all the information out due to children being involved at that time, but I could care less how the adult in this situation looks. After seeing the things I saw, I have zero sympathy for this lady, NONE!!! It really showed the maturity level of this so-called woman and that was all I needed to see. It was a wrap from there! There are receipts below!

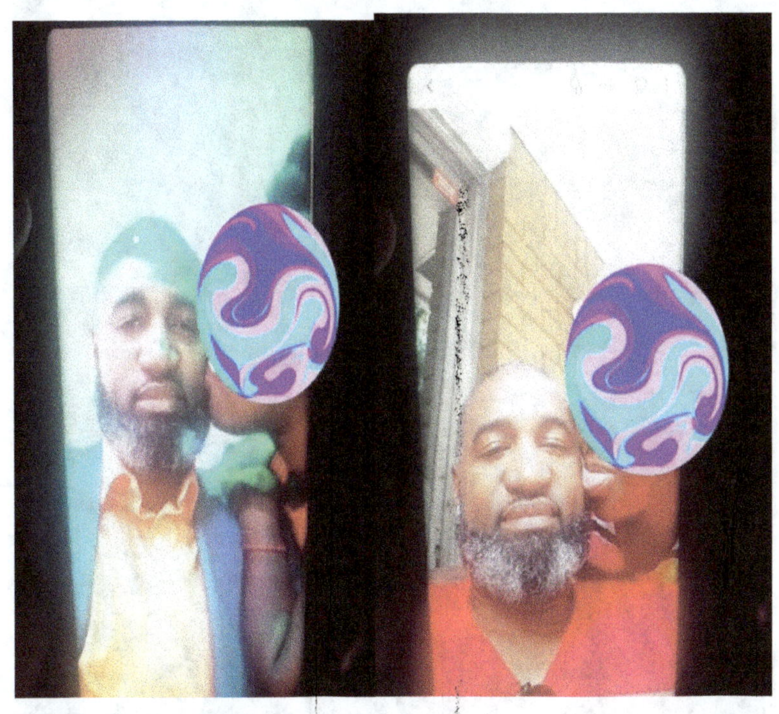

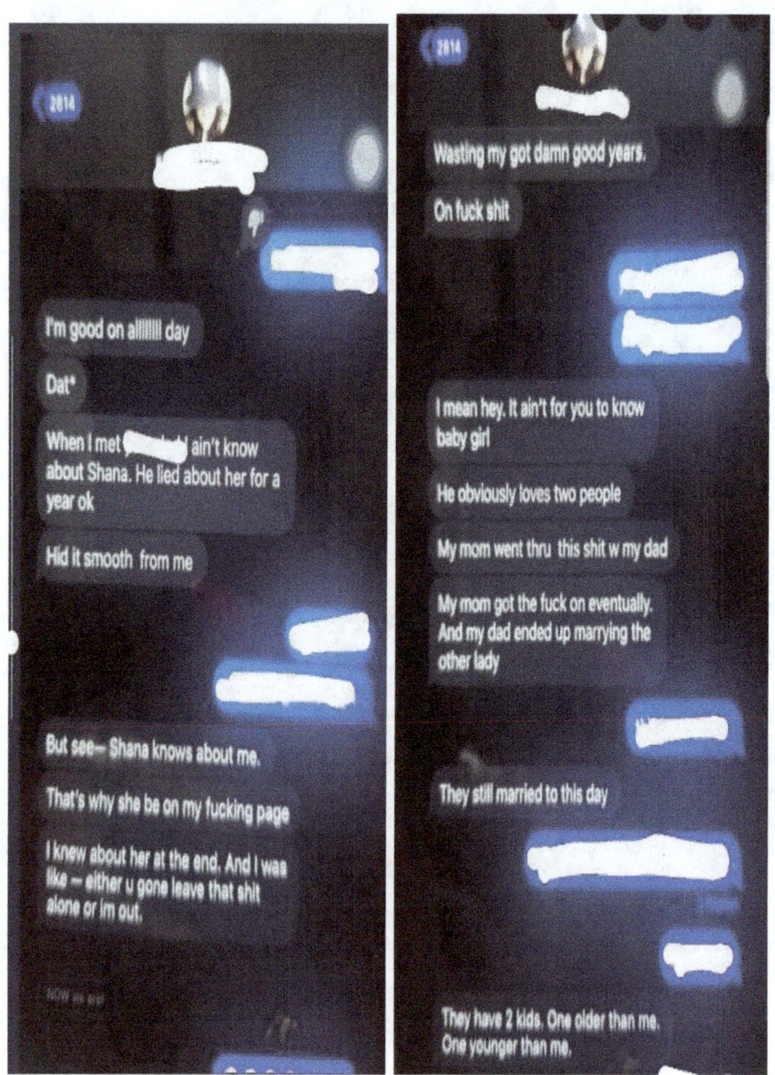
I'm good on allllll day

Dat*

When I met ████████ I ain't know about Shana. He lied about her for a year ok

Hid it smooth from me

But see— Shana knows about me.

That's why she be on my fucking page

I knew about her at the end. And I was like — either u gone leave that shit alone or im out.

Wasting my got damn good years.

On fuck shit

I mean hey. It ain't for you to know baby girl

He obviously loves two people

My mom went thru this shit w my dad

My mom got the fuck on eventually. And my dad ended up marrying the other lady

They still married to this day

They have 2 kids. One older than me. One younger than me.

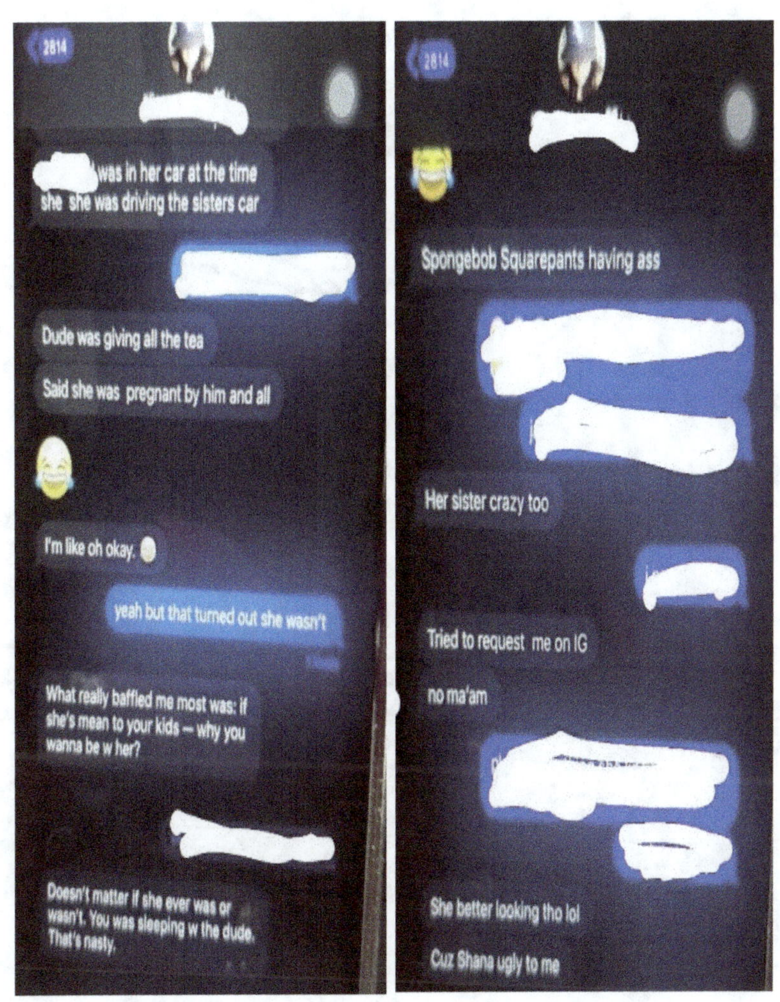
was in her car at the time
she she was driving the sisters car

Dude was giving all the tea

Said she was pregnant by him and all

I'm like oh okay.

yeah but that turned out she wasn't

What really baffled me most was: if
she's mean to your kids — why you
wanna be w her?

Doesn't matter if she ever was or
wasn't. You was sleeping w the dude.
That's nasty.

Spongebob Squarepants having ass

Her sister crazy too

Tried to request me on IG

no ma'am

She better looking tho lol

Cuz Shana ugly to me

CHAPTER 7

Still Trying To Be There

Harry Was Torn

As I was adding upgrades to my home, Harry and his brother Larry used to stop by to visit with me and the kids all the time. They would sit and eat or have a glass of wine. When they left, Larry would question Harry, asking, "What are you doing?" He would advise him to stop playing games and going back and forth. "It's not healthy and that's why you're so stressed out".

Larry explained to me that, with everything Harry had done with this lady and all she had done for him, he couldn't just come back right away. He owed her and was afraid to hurt her. He was afraid of what his friends would think of him. I take nothing away from what she had done for him at all, but I have no respect for whatever they had going on.

I remember a conversation Larry told me he had with Harry when he was visiting their home. Harry walked into the room where Larry was, laid across the bed, and started talking about me. He wasn't sure why he was hurting me or why he was doing what he was doing. His brother told him his heart wasn't where he was laying his head, and it was with me. Harry didn't deny it. Instead, he dropped his head and said nothing! Larry said until you're real with yourself, you can't be real with anyone, not this lady or Shana. He said your body is here, but your heart isn't. Harry agreed, there was pure silence! That was something I already knew from day one. No one will ever convince me otherwise.

She was in Harry's life for the reason God placed her there, in his time of need. I believe that he fell for her based on everything she had done for him. He needed both of us and he wasn't willing to let me go be happy, like I had asked him to because he loved us both… just in different ways and for different reasons.

While Harry battled the cancer, he wanted me to still be there for him. He would call his brother at 3am talking about me. There were times when Harry would call and find out that I wasn't home, and he would ride by my house. Damn right… I wasn't there! He lived with another woman. Why would I be home waiting on him? Larry even said at one point the lady told him, "If you want to go back there, that's fine… Go"; but at that point he knew I was basically over it and wasn't welcoming him back into my home to rebuild our relationship. The only thing I was concerned with was nurturing our friendship, so she was all he had to fall back on. Our time had passed.

Since his heart was with me, he continued to make promises to move out; but he and a few of his siblings told me that he reaped the benefits of living with her. She was helping him, and he loved that lifestyle she provided for him. He was a very flashy person. I loved him but I wasn't doing all of that for him - especially after what he had taken me through. He claimed to be charging credit cards left and right, free flights, his car note paid and car insurance after I canceled him from my policy in 2021.

She would take Harry out of town and of course he tried to hide it from me. I wasn't questioning that man. If that's what he wanted to do, I just let him! He loved that lifestyle. If he liked it, I loved it! I continued to see him because I wanted to believe in him. I still had hopes that he was being genuine for the sake of our friendship.

Harry had his chemo sessions every other Thursday. Afterwards, he and I saw each other like clockwork. I would cook for him, and he would rest in my bed until he went back to her home. He would always send me songs to listen to, expressing how he felt. Three songs that stood out were *"Finding my way back"* by Jaheim, *"Holding on"* by Greg Porter and Kem and *"Don't take your love away"* by Avant. He sent me so many songs, but these are the three he said he always thought of when he thought about us. It was his way of getting his feelings out, I suppose. Was it right, probably not, but the same way you get a man is normally how you lose him. Since he wasn't married to her or me, I guess it went both ways and that's the reason she kept seeing him after knowing he was in a relationship with me for years.

3:38   59%

< **Harry**
+14049365321   **Delete all**

Friday, July 30, 2021

What

Whatever 5:44 PM

Really 6:10 PM

Love u too 7:42 PM

U dont deserve anything of thus matter. Guess u out with some nigga trying to pay me back whenbu have it all wrong 10:09 PM

Saturday, July 31, 2021

We will talk ok 2:16 AM

We will be well 6:19 PM

U wanna leave it aint happening 6:52 PM

Now u on some old new shit 7:07 PM

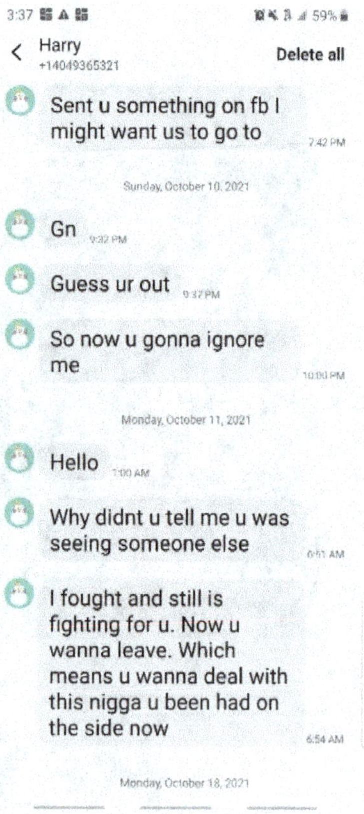

3:37   59%

< **Harry**
+14049365321   **Delete all**

Sent u something on fb I might want us to go to 7:42 PM

Sunday, October 10, 2021

Gn 9:32 PM

Guess ur out 9:37 PM

So now u gonna ignore me 10:00 PM

Monday, October 11, 2021

Hello 1:00 AM

Why didnt u tell me u was seeing someone else 6:51 AM

I fought and still is fighting for u. Now u wanna leave. Which means u wanna deal with this nigga u been had on the side now 6:54 AM

Monday, October 18, 2021

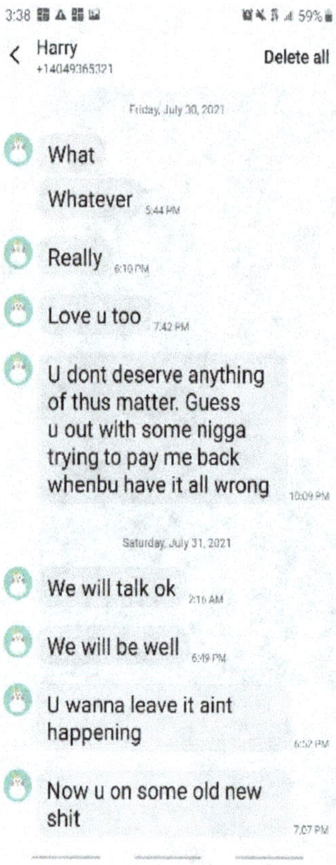

Financial Hardship

There were a lot of things I continued to help Harry with because I still believed what he was telling me, and I wanted to help him. He was no longer getting income and was past due on several things. I told him he would need to ask the lady he lived with to help pay his bills. I only agreed to keep him on my car insurance from 2/2020 until 7/2021. Basically, two years or so after he moved. I didn't know in 2020 that he lived with anyone other than a former neighbor he had me to believe. So, I continued to keep him on my car insurance policy because I felt bad for him and he asked me to not give up on him. I didn't at that time because I wasn't ready to.

He hit a deer this same year and damaged the car badly. I set everything up to have the car dropped off at the collision center and met his brother, Larry to pick the car up in Conyers after it was finished because he had just had another procedure and couldn't come up there to get the truck. I also helped him get a loan for 30k because he kept talking about not having income. He wanted to start a business due to not having income coming in so he could still leave something behind for his children. Do you think any of those funds came to my household? Nope, but I wasn't looking for that. Once again he gave a date for when he wanted to come back. That conversation went in one ear and out the other. Was it smart, of course not, why did I do it? Because I didn't want to give up on him. I had his back and I wanted to be there for him and trust and believe I was!

The Hard Questions

In October of 2021, a letter came from the hospital that he worked at. It stated that he was separated from the company. This meant he lost all benefits as far as health and life insurance policies etc. This was a shocker. When it came, I immediately sent him a picture, so he knew the letter came in October. I'm not sure why he didn't act on it then and seek additional coverage. I think it wasn't until 2022 when he really started looking for more coverage. This is when he began to ask me for help with locating him some life insurance policies. Many asked if I had a life insurance policy on him. The answer is yes, I did but I canceled it when he moved out. There was no need in me keeping it on him, I really wish I did though. If I would've kept it, I would've given the money to his kids because they deserved it. He knew I was working on my business, and I also was an insurance agent with a good friend of his at that time. Being that he had stage 4 cancer there were very few to no life insurance companies that would accept him. I told him to ask his friend since he was in that business way longer than I had been. He said he asked him, and he was working on it for him as well. I really wanted to help him, but I was speaking to someone, and they stated if he was to get life insurance, he would have to be alive at least two years after the policy would originate. I even tried to do this but the policy I tried to help him get, denied him. I was there for him and helping him every step of the way trying to make sure he didn't have to worry about things but there was only so much I could've done. As I have said… on so many levels… I stayed by his side until the end!

If You Don't Make Decisions, Decisions Will Be Made For You

Not Tying Up Loose Ends

Until this day, all his mail still came to my house. He even received a 15-year plaque, cup, and pin that I sent to his children. I'm not sure why, when he moved, he never changed his address. I felt like that was his duty to do, since he was not here. I kept asking him to switch it, but he never did. He kept saying he didn't want to, and everything was how it needed to be. So, I left it like that! I was speaking to a friend/cousin of his named Dilan, and we were just talking about him and the decisions he has made. His friend was disappointed in him because he left so much undone without facing it. A few of his friends tried talking to him when he was in hospice about his wishes and just in general about what he wanted. He kept blowing them off. He was dodging the conversation and reality of his condition.

His friend Dilan also told me that Harry showed him a ring that he had for me. This wasn't the first time I was told about this ring, so

I knew it was true. Dilan told me he told Harry to do right and marry me and stop playing around; But like I told Dilan, he wasn't ready for marriage and the time for a proposal is when things are going well - not when you've already lost the person you love.

My best friend, Lisa, sat with him on many occasions, some occasions I wasn't even aware of until after the fact. She also said he showed her the ring and the receipt on when he purchased it, around the time I had already checked out. I was shocked but not so much because he did things like this to reel me back in and try to make things right after the damage was already done.

My daughter even said that she and the other kids saw the ring. He showed the kids when I told him it was over. I spoke with him about it later in 2021 and he did confirm he did have a ring. I told him if we were in a better place, I would've considered it but so much had happened that I was not marrying a man who couldn't change his ways. He had developed a new relationship with someone else who he cared for and I was not sharing him no matter what his condition was!

Relationship Is Over

I had boundaries and I stuck to them in the end. I'm glad I did although he wasn't happy about this. He thought it would be okay for me to stay with him while he continued to be there due to his illness. That was never something I would agree to but just because the relationship was over didn't mean I couldn't be there as his friend, and I was!

During this time, I had a strong support system. I had my former coworker and friend Kayla and Shamika who helped me with the healing process and figuring out how to handle and deal with moving forward. I had serval friends that were there for me through this process and helped in a multitude of ways. From listening to me vent, offering advice, inviting me to events to stay busy and suggesting healing methods to keep my mental aligned. Thank you ladies and gents! Lisa, Maggie, Nia, Sherri, and his brother Larry. You guys were the reason I pulled it together and moved TF on!

I saw Harry up until September of 2021. I ended the relationship on any level other than being there for him as a friend. To be honest, as far as the relationship was concerned, I had been checked out from that. It just wasn't cut off sexually and that was my choice to make.

For the nosey people in the back, yes! We stayed intimate until 2021. It was never cut off when he moved out. Once again, he wasn't married to me or this lady. My relationship wasn't respected so I wasn't respecting whatever he had going on over that way! However, I finally stopped him from popping up. I changed my locks and finally started to date again in 2021. I explained to Harry that what we had was officially over, and he had to stop all the visits and pop ups. I ended all of that in 2021. He did try it a few times in 2022; but eventually he got the picture and stopped. I wasn't trying to hurt him, but I had to show him that it was really over. He couldn't have me in that aspect anymore. Besides, he had someone for that.

He sent me some hurtful things when I first did it; but later apologized and told me he was hurt and that's why he lashed out on me after finding out I had moved on and started dating. I had to make a drastic move, so he knew I was serious about just remaining friends with him and I did!

The love I shared with that man kept me accepting things I don't believe I would have accepted from anyone else while we were together, but it also created a bond and friendship that lasted beyond his passing. A friendship that outlasted my desire to be with him and even his poor decisions and messed up behavior. I was a true friend to him, one who really looked after his wellbeing… unconditionally. I loved Harry in spite of himself and that's something no rumor can tarnish!

Rebuilding, Reshaping, and Cleansing My Life

*J*n September of 2021, I joined an app and started dating. This was the first time I ever considered doing this. I was tired of the same old way of meeting people such as at the bars, in the stores, or just out. This was different but I said, *what the heck... why not give it a try.* It was an app that allowed the ladies to run things, in a sense. If you liked or saw interest in a guy you swiped right. If you didn't you swiped left. If that guy swiped right as well then you two were a match and the woman would message the guy first. I was okay with that. I met Juan online that same month that I joined, and we went back and forth getting to know each other.

In the beginning, I was kind of hesitant because his bio information said he didn't know what he wanted. He was fresh out of a relationship, so he really wasn't sure if he wanted to get back into one or remain single. Now normally, if I see someone's bio that says they are not sure of what they want, I move right on; but for some reason a voice in my head said just wait and see how it goes. So, I did just that.

After a few dates, I was really interested. We started going over our likes and dislikes and seemed to be a great match. I enjoyed being around him. In October, he asked me if we could make this thing official and we did.

I vowed to start the relationship off right and be honest about everything, which is the same thing I had done in my last relationship. There is no doubt that I had been hurt in the past, so I vowed that I wouldn't carry my past pain on into the next relationship. These were two different men and I made sure I kept reminding myself of just that. He knew coming into this, everything I did and what my ex had done as well. I was not going to tell half-truths. We both were the cause of the demise of the relationship, and I wanted to be the change I had been expecting. So, I held nothing back.

In June 2022, my daughter and I sat with Juan, and I told him that I was always going to be there for Harry's children if they ever needed me since they were close to me and my children. He was very open and didn't have an issue with that at all. This is what I loved about him. He was a friend first and we could openly talk to each other about anything.

Moving Forward – Hospital Visits

His brother Larry was visiting him in the hospital, and he said that Harry wanted to have a talk about everything dealing with him. Since he was the only one there, Larry wasn't sure when the talk would take place but he said he asked him when they would talk. Harry kept putting it off saying he was tired and on his meds - making more excuses. Larry stated that more people started arriving. His former coworkers and a few other home boys of his and then the lady he had been with came in and says she didn't want Harry to get covid so some of the people might need to leave. Larry says he ended up leaving without speaking to his brother like they had agreed to. The talk about his wishes or what should happen going forward never happened.

Hospice Care

On June 16, 2022, I found out he was in hospice from a good friend from South Carolina.

She had been updating me on his status when I didn't hear from him at times. She was in communication with her cousin who was close to the lady's cousin. A day later, I had to let him know I knew where he was, and I wanted to come see him. He agreed and apologized for not telling me sooner but told me he wanted to see me before anything happened to him.

On June 17th, I went to see Harry in hospice. I took him a sweet card from my heart and a balloon. His brother's former girlfriend, accompanied me on the visit. She left us in the room about an hour before coming in. I held his hand and prayed over him. Then, I asked him if his affairs were in order. He said, "Yes, you know my ex-wife is handling everything with me." I said, "Okay, good." We spoke about this in the past, so I knew he wanted her to handle things dealing with him due to the field in which she worked.

He was watching TV as we were talking. I told him I didn't come up there to watch him watch TV. He turned around to me and said out of nowhere, "I'm so sorry for everything I took you through and for lying for so long". He told me he wanted to come back but wasn't sure I could care for him like he needed me to. I told him I understood why he stayed and that I was glad he had someone there for him that had the knowledge and experience to care for him. I told him that I was thankful he had the professional homecare there for him. He shed a tear and looked away. I knew he was hurting, and I said to him I was sorry for how everything went in the past and for hurting him. "We are now both set free from our past and everything that happened." I said and told him that God performs miracles daily and to keep talking to God. "Either way this goes, just know I've always been there for you and love you." I said to him, "God is a forgiving God, Harry, and he has already forgiven you". Harry thanked me and we both cried. I hugged and kissed his forehead. It was a special moment!

His best friend and former classmate and his wife from South Carolina entered the room and they began their visit with him. I gave him another hug he kissed my cheek and I left. That was the last time I saw him. I was at peace; and listening to him talk to his friends, he was in a happier mood from when I first got there. So, I knew then God had forgiven us both for how we hurt each other in the past.

On June 29th, Harry advised me that he was leaving hospice and going home for hospice care. He said he had been throwing up due to some pills that were given to him by the nurse which were supposed to dissolve. It was hard for him to take the pills at this point, he stated with the port running through his nose. Eventually, they released him. They didn't want to send him home with the port going through his nose so that was the hold up on being released. On June 30th, he was getting settled in, with home care hospice. On July 2nd, he was getting his vitals check and taking meds; this was the last message I received from him.

The Last Time Hearing From Him

July 6th was the last update I received before his passing. I got a message from someone close to him, saying he sends his love to me and that he has lost his vision and hearing and not ignoring my messages. After getting this, I broke down. I was okay after he left hospice, but it was getting real from that day forward because I knew in my heart he was transitioning. All the praying I had done, I knew then. God spoke to me and said this is it. I stopped texting and calling since I knew he couldn't respond back. Until this day, his messages were being read and he was actively responding and updating me every step of the way. He was very guarded, and something he promised me was that he wouldn't give anyone access to his phone to view our private messages we shared. Especially, anyone with ill intentions anyway. He kept that promise!

Harry passed away on July 20, 2022. I was at work that morning when I got the call from his sibling. I immediately left to go home to tell my daughter. My son was at work. I had to tell them before they heard it somewhere else. He was like a second father to them. My daughter cried for about an hour and I held her trying to console her. This was so heartbreaking. My children were very close to him. He was around them and helped raise them, so this loss was deep for us. Yes, their fathers were active in their lives, but Harry was like a father to them and he was there for them as well.

7/27/2022 Viewing Lithonia, GA

A lot of my close friends and family who knew him came out to support and view his body. He knew so many people and was a very social being. He had a good heart and meant well; tried to help everyone he knew. Although I was at peace with everything after we had our moment in hospice, it still hurt my heart to see him in that casket. He had his flaws and wasn't always honest about everything; but he didn't deserve his life ending so soon. God just had other plans for him, and it was his time. No more pain, as I see it. He fought until the end, and he was called home. In the hospice bed, I knew he had been talking to God and was forgiven for everything. I was happy about that. He deserved peace in the end when God called him home.

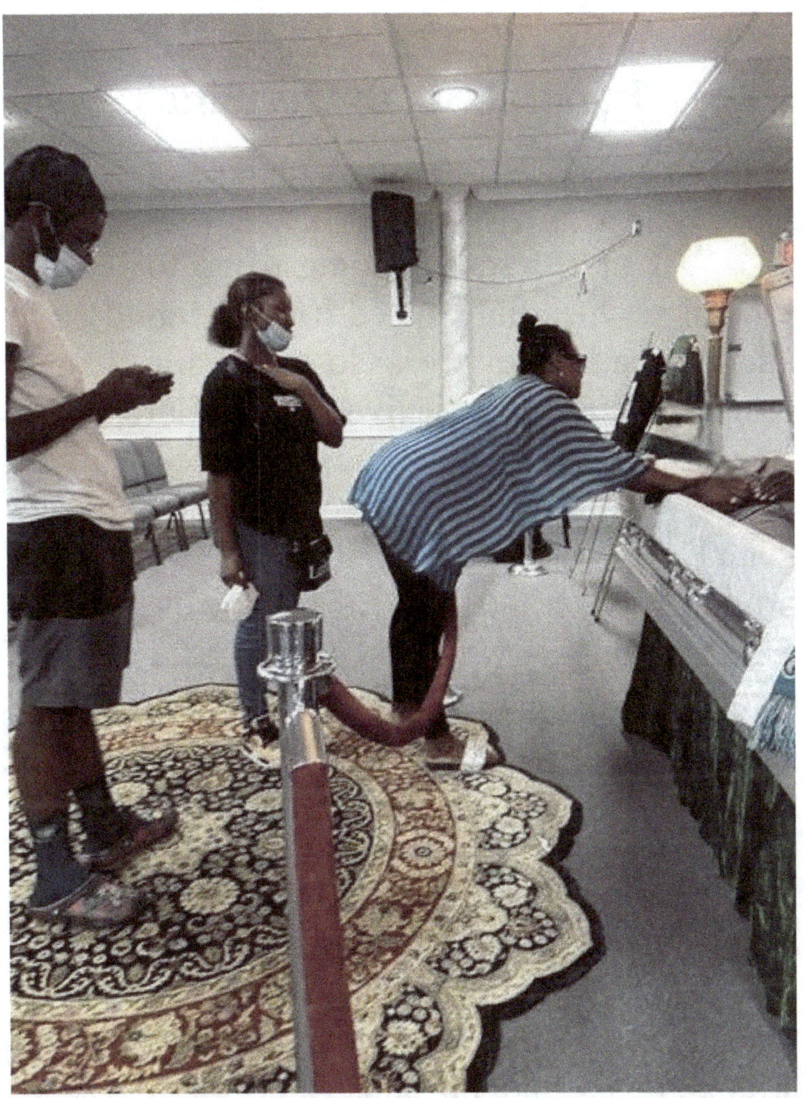

Funeral Services
7/27/2022
Funeral South Carolina

At first, I wasn't going to go to Harry's funeral service, but I owed it to my children to attend because they were close to him and knew him nine years of their lives. My children and I went to South Carolina and we stayed with his brother. While we were there, we spent time and talked with his friend Dilan. Two of his other brothers, James and Cody, also came over. It was a good night, we were just getting ready for the next day and catching up. We stayed up talking about Harry and some of the good times we all had with him. Little did I know, only one of his siblings would attend his homegoing service and later I realized why. The funeral was not what Harry wanted. While he was in hospice, he specifically told me that he wanted his ex-wife to oversee everything regarding his funeral arrangements and he chose her for a reason. Harry wanted to be in the same city as his small children; but when you leave things unwritten and not in order, things are done the way others want them done, versus how you wanted them. *When you don't make decisions, decisions will be made for you.* This is why people should have their affairs in order before it's too late. I won't discuss all the details, but I do know that he didn't have a life insurance policy outside of his job due to the loss of his job in October of 2021.

That means there was no money to bury him officially at that point. I know this because the mail from Harry never stopped coming to my home. I'm glad that everyone who loved him came together to bury him. I would have pitched in, but no one ever reached out to me regarding contributing anything, and I was okay with that. I had my peace when I saw him in hospice. Because Harry did not have his affairs in order, decisions were made for him. His body was taken to South Carolina and his request for his ex-wife, who is in the funeral business, to be the overseer of the funeral arrangement was disregarded. A few of his aunts on both his dad and mom's sides attended the services but for the most part, only one sibling, two cousins, and friends were in attendance. Another brother came to the burial site but wasn't at the funeral. Once again, when you don't make decisions, decisions are made for you.

After his passing, I received a letter from his job, stating he had something in place called the survivor benefits package and benefit payments from his former policy. This was the remaining funds from a plan he had with his job. So, what did I do with that money?

What do you think...? The right thing.

Harry had mentioned to me that when it's all said and done, I would see how he truly felt about me, and I did. I reached out to the children's mother and turned it over to her. He was their dad and they deserved every bit of the money, if not more. Harry spoke loud and clear from death – what he wanted and how he felt! Thanks for keeping your word in the end with that!

In April of the year following his death, a letter came in the mail which was dated for 3/15/2023. It was from the retirement department at his hospital job. I supposed someone contacted them to change his address. They had my address listed in the letter as well as the address where he was staying at with the lady. There was a change in address from mine to hers. Harry has passed on almost a year now so I'm not sure what the reason for switching it over now was unless someone is looking for something more to come. Hopefully, it wasn't his benefits package because that was where it belonged… with his kids!

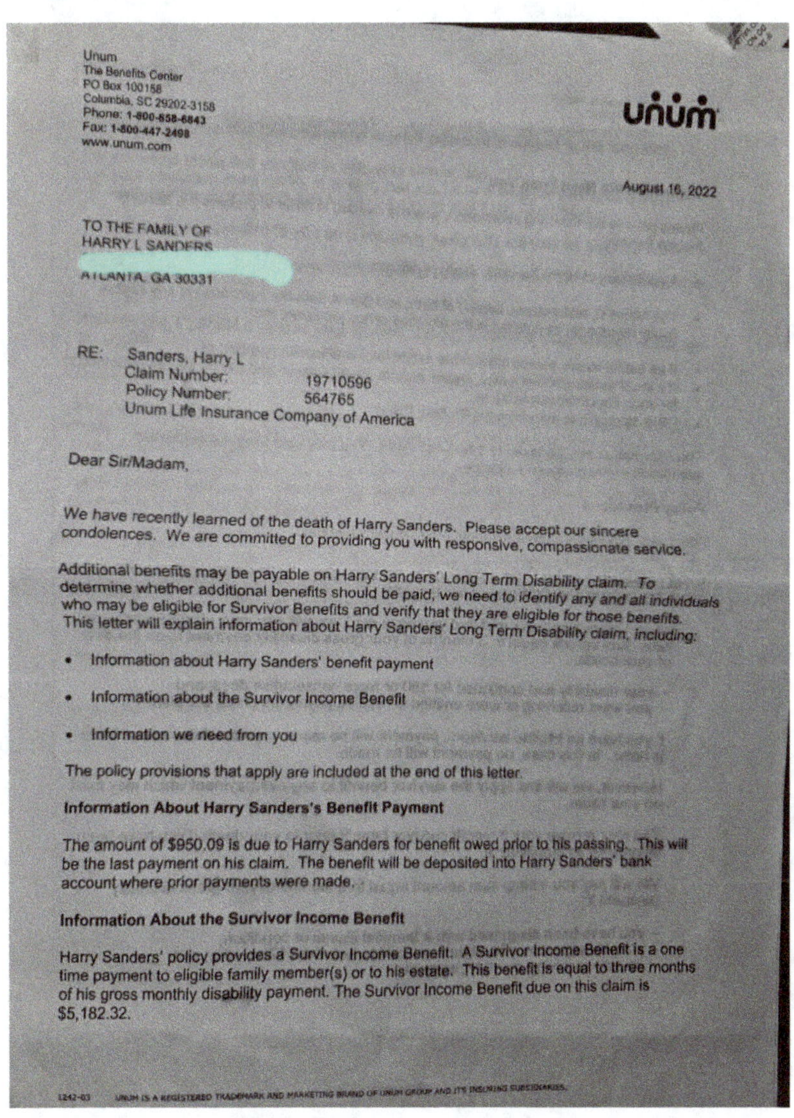

Unum
The Benefits Center
PO Box 100158
Columbia, SC 29202-3158
Phone: 1-800-858-6843
Fax: 1-800-447-2498
www.unum.com

unum

August 16, 2022

TO THE FAMILY OF
HARRY L SANDERS

ATLANTA, GA 30331

RE: Sanders, Harry L
       Claim Number: 19710596
       Policy Number: 564765
       Unum Life Insurance Company of America

Dear Sir/Madam,

We have recently learned of the death of Harry Sanders. Please accept our sincere condolences. We are committed to providing you with responsive, compassionate service.

Additional benefits may be payable on Harry Sanders' Long Term Disability claim. To determine whether additional benefits should be paid, we need to identify any and all individuals who may be eligible for Survivor Benefits and verify that they are eligible for those benefits. This letter will explain information about Harry Sanders' Long Term Disability claim, including:

- Information about Harry Sanders' benefit payment

- Information about the Survivor Income Benefit

- Information we need from you

The policy provisions that apply are included at the end of this letter.

Information About Harry Sanders's Benefit Payment

The amount of $950.09 is due to Harry Sanders for benefit owed prior to his passing. This will be the last payment on his claim. The benefit will be deposited into Harry Sanders' bank account where prior payments were made.

Information About the Survivor Income Benefit

Harry Sanders' policy provides a Survivor Income Benefit. A Survivor Income Benefit is a one time payment to eligible family member(s) or to his estate. This benefit is equal to three months of his gross monthly disability payment. The Survivor Income Benefit due on this claim is $5,182.32.

L242-03   UNUM IS A REGISTERED TRADEMARK AND MARKETING BRAND OF UNUM GROUP AND ITS INSURING SUBSIDIARIES.

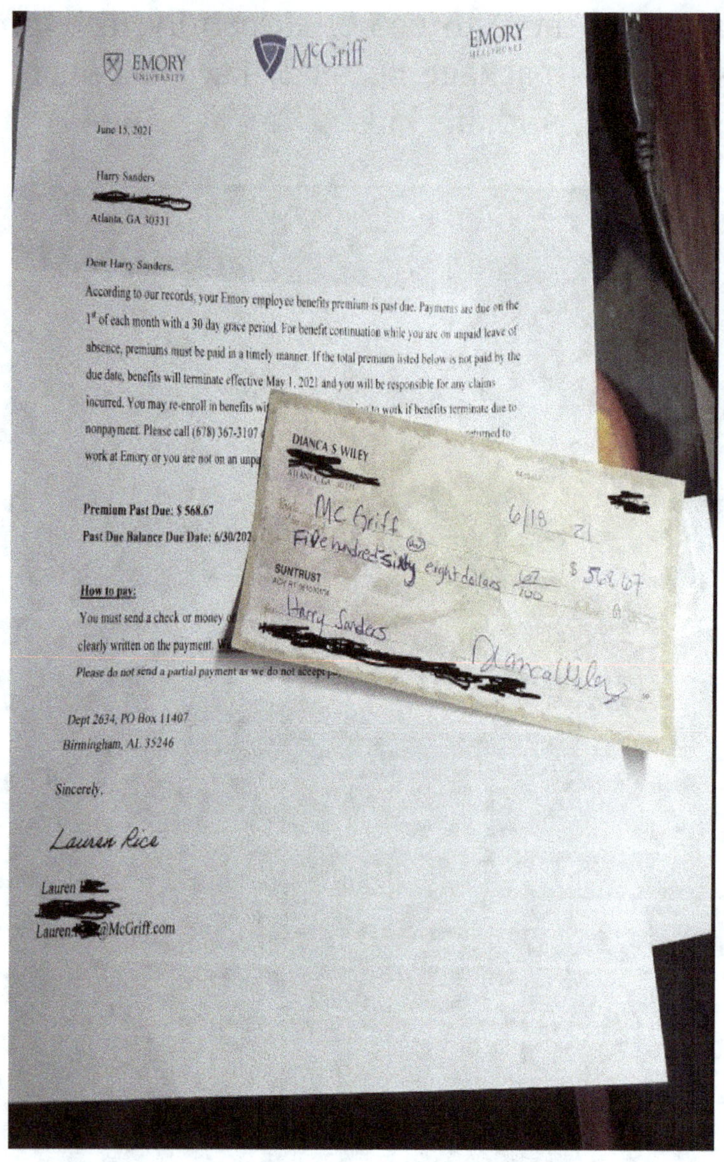

← **Your Daily Digest for Tue, May 23**

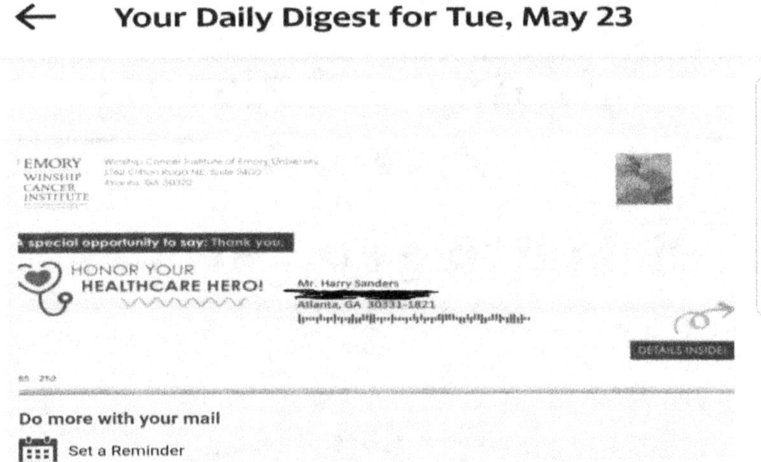

Do more with your mail

Set a Reminder

Grieving and Moving Forward

Rebuilding and Healing

This May Hurt A Few Feelings
Last Wishes

After speaking with Harry over the years, especially while he was in hospice, I asked him if his affairs were in order regarding the burial and funeral etc. Several others close to him had similar conversations with him about this too. Everyone knew he wanted his ex-wife, who was also the mother of his children to oversee all of his affairs dealing with his final arrangements. After I asked him about his affairs being in order, he said, "You know my ex-wife is in charge of all of that". Harry went on to say, "I want to be buried here with my kids" and that's all I will say about that.

Regardless of how anyone feels, his ex-wife was the woman who Harry was with for years. No one knew him like she did; especially not the woman who was with him for the last few years of his life. No one knew him like the woman that saw him in the good, the bad, the angry, the sad, the hurt, the flashy, the tantrum throwing and on top of that, at his lowest. The one he laid next to, telling his secrets to, revealing his hurt from his childhood, and explaining why it was so hard to open up the first few years of the relationship. *That woman was me… And that's just facts.* Take it how you want. This is my truth, and I can't open up any more than I have.

After He Passes

I received multiple calls requesting that I keep his secrets private. Why would I hold in his secrets when some of it caused me so much pain publicly? People need to be told the truth and not just have the "A man will be a man" mentality! No, if you love or care for someone and you see them not doing right or hurting someone or playing games, why ignore it and go on with it? Many people say, "it's not your business" but if you're close to that person in any way, it is your business to tell them the truth whether right or wrong.

I received so many positive messages and inspirational videos from members of Harry's family. His cousins, aunts, and siblings – everyone knew what I meant to Harry and how close he was to me in life and in his last days. For them to send those special messages, meant a lot to me because I already knew what they were telling me… to be his truth. There were a few who made attempts to downgrade the role I played in his life, but truth be told… it was bigger than anyone of them probably ever knew.

I know what role I played in Harry's life and so did he and that's all that mattered.

This book wasn't written to expose Harry and what he was doing because everyone already knew that – it was no secret. The purpose of this book was to shed light on just how much I was there for him regardless of where he was or what anyone had to say or think.

I got sent a post of someone who barely knew him, saying that this lady "was the only one he loved!!!"

Like really? That is a fat ass lie!!! If that were the case, he would have focused on what he had over there with her and stopped coming over or communicating with me daily just to tell me how he felt. Harry was a charmer and a socialite. He was the life of the party; hell… he was the party. There were things he wasn't ready to face and being truthful and hurting the feelings of some of those who loved him were just a few things he was battling with.

Mental health is real, and it damages a person starting from childhood. This type of trauma stays with you. It festers and is carried into adulthood; sometimes, unidentified. Harry faced several challenges in life and unfortunately it carried over into his adulthood and had him second guessing people in his life who were genuinely there. With everything that this lady had done for him, of course he wasn't going to let that go; but if he had his way- he would have had us both. He wasn't having me on the side, I just wasn't going for that. Still, I stood by him until the end as a friend, like I promised him I would. He couldn't make the decision for himself, so I chose to make it for him.

Regardless of what you have heard or been told, I ended the relationship because mentally it was draining. It was too much to carry. He was battling for his life, yet he stayed doing things he shouldn't have been doing. This needed to stop, his health should have been more of a priority sooner than it was; but he didn't seem to take it seriously until it was too late. Doing what he was doing would stress anyone out. Instead of him focusing on Harry, he was trying to satisfy everyone. Harry had a mind of his own and no one could change his mind but him. He made his own choices and ultimately, he had to deal with the result of those choices he made. He chose to neglect the most important choices and it ended with those choices being made for him. God has him now, he made it right for those who mattered to him in the end and that's all that matters!

The Start To My Happiness

$\mathcal{I}$ started a new relationship with Juan about a little over a year before Harry had passed. Juan was very supportive with me and my children attending the funeral. That was all I needed to see from this man, that was it for me. We met September 12, 2021, on a dating app. Neither one of us had been on a dating app before, so this was new to us both.

In the beginning, Juan didn't know what he wanted but I knew I wanted a serious relationship. Even though he was unsure, I didn't count him out. We continued to talk and chat, until we finally went on a date. A few dates later it felt like we would always be around each other. Juan figured out very quickly what he wanted and that was me! We started officially dating on October 20, 2021, only a month later, as an official couple. This man has been everything he told me he would be. I finally have someone in my corner who truly loves me and shows it daily. We have done so much within the first year of knowing each other. He is the first man to attend church with me. He is the first man I ever traveled outside the US with. We have gone out the country three times and traveled on vacation over 12 times. This is everything I needed. He came into my life at a time when I needed the comfort. He has treated my children like they are his own and that is a blessing within itself.

On February 11, 2023, I reserved a hotel for a work event we were attending. We celebrated his birthday that Friday and attended the banquet that Saturday. He was late getting there and that's normally not his style, but I ignored it and tried not to make it a big deal. After the night was almost over, he kept rushing to leave and I wondered why he was rushing. Little did I know, when we get back to the room this man had it decorated and ask me to be his wife. I had no idea he would do it that night. I was so shocked. I wanted to cry but he told me not to. God brought us together.

We started talking about when we wanted the special day to be. We were discussing why not do it on his birthday. So yes, we officially got married on February 14, 2023. We decided to still have the full wedding a year later, set for February 10, 2024, and plan to announce it there to all our family and friends. This is how we wanted it and I'm glad we did it this way. In the end it's about our happiness and I'm so glad we found each other and now we are doing this thing called life together.

There was a time when I prayed for this kind of love but almost believe I might not ever experience it. That goes to show you that you never know what God's plan is. I learned a lot about myself from my relationship with Harry. I learned a lot more about life from the way he lived and died. Life is really so short and we all have to do what's best for each and every one of us. Just make sure you are valuing what's really important because you never know what's ahead for you in God's plan. My story is still being written so stay tuned for more happiness and love from my family to yours.

CHAPTER 12

CLOSING

This book is about my life, it's about forgiveness, wisdom, happiness, heartache and love… but most of all it's about awareness. I am grateful for every lesson I learned while I went through this process. If I didn't go through this, I wouldn't know what it truly feels like to be in love with your best friend who will always have your back no matter what; and I wouldn't have had a real life example of how important it is to get your final affairs in order(in writing).

Life is about trials and tribulations we must face and go through to come out on top. I prayed to God so many nights asking, "why me? Why do I have to endure all this hurt and pain?" God responded saying, "why not you?" He chose me to go through this and all along, I was being tested. Trust the process and the path that has been placed in front of you. You never know what may be at the end of the path. Your light is waiting for you and watch how you shine once you trust the process. I'm so glad I didn't give up on myself or my life. God had bigger and better waiting!!!!

Life Beyond Today is a book filled with the experiences and life lessons I was faced with. It shows you all about the big lessons I learned in love; but the biggest lesson in this story was learned through Harry. Harry didn't have his affairs in order or lined up, so his wishes couldn't be upheld. You never want it to where family and friends are bickering over what you would have wanted when this could have been all avoided if you only took a few moments to get things written out before you transitioned.

Life Beyond Today as a business was created and formed for people to have a safe place to store their documents and have their beneficiary have direct access to their information. If anything was to happen to that person, where they could not speak for themselves, the beneficiary can come back to my company and get all the documents they provided to the platform. These documents could be a variety of things, a will, trust funds, 401k information, list of active bank accounts, attorney information, power of attorney information, and variety of other things your loved ones could use to speak on your behalf.

People should think about not only their lives as of today but beyond today! They should think about their loved ones and how their lives ending will affect them. Don't let your story end with someone else making your decisions! Take the necessary steps to decide for yourself and make life beyond today easier for those you love.

Visit the website for more information on how Life Beyond Today can get and keep affairs in order, for you and your family!

For more estate planning:

www.lifebeyondtodayllc.com

Shana's

List of Important Final Documents

After you have passed it is too late to set up your final arrangements or get your final affairs in order. Leaving these tasks unaddressed can lead to bickering and added stress for your loved ones. These are a few of the documents you need to have in order so that everything will go as you have planned it in the event of your transitioning.

✓ **Living Will/ Will**
✓ **Power of Attorney**
✓ **Deeds** to any properties you own
✓ **Titles** to all vehicles you own

These are just a few of the documents necessary for the proper transfer of your estate after your passing. Find a full list on my website!

SELF-CARE TIPS

After the Divorce, Breakup or Traumatic Relationship:

❧ Give yourself some space. You don't need to shut your ex out of your life especially if kids are involved. But it might be helpful to try to avoid the person for a while after the break-up. Move out. Stop attending similar hang outs, etc. This means having connections with them online too.

❧ Stay busy! You might find yourself with a lot of free time on your hands, especially on weekends. Plan activities ahead and do things that you enjoy with friends and family.

❧ Work on self-care. Take time to do things for yourself. Do relaxing things, like the spa, nails, hair, massages, and a nice getaway, watching a movie, enjoying some music, or exercising.

❧ Talk to family, friends, spiritual advisors, therapist, and others who can support you. It's OK to want some time to yourself but having the supportive people at hand, helps keep your mind off things and can help give you a different perspective.

❧ Try not to use alcohol and other drugs to deal with the pain. While they might help you feel better at first, the after-effects can leave you feeling much worse, and the pain will still be there in the end.

❧ Give yourself time to heal. Allow yourself time to adjust to the new reality after the breakup. Don't rush into another relationship. Heal first!

∞ Try to keep yourself in good shape and stay healthy. Taking vitamins, eating healthy remain active with working out, getting a lot of rest and everything needed to keep yourself right not only on the outside but the inside as well.

❧ Feeling down or depressed won't last forever. It will take some time to get thru it and process the situation and accept the reality. You will have good days and then there will be sad days. Get through them and be ready for the next day.

❧ If you ended the relationship this doesn't make it easier. If they ended the relationship doesn't mean that you lack anything thereof. Don't take it personal because this happens all the time. You may not have been the right fit for that person, but you will be the right fit for your soulmate.

❧ It is better to not be in a relationship than to continue being in an unhealthy relationship.

❧ Always respect the person's decision if they no longer want to continue the relationship. It makes it much easier to accept it and move on than bicker and argue on things that no longer matter.

❧ You do not need a relationship to be happy.

❧ Respect boundaries if someone ended the relationship and you also should demand boundaries from the other person if you end it. If you continue to go back and forth with someone, they will never respect your decision or you.

❧ Never get to a place where it turns angry or toxic. Feelings are better expressed when it's done in a healthy matter without toxic methods.

❧ Never feel embarrassed about ending a relationship and how it looks in the eyes of others. No one is in the relationship but you and the other person. Who cares what others think. You will feel more embarrassed by staying in an unhealthy relationship for years and years to come, rather than separating or divorcing after years of pretending and doing what looked right in the world's eyes, rather than what was right and what you needed to make you happy.

❧ Try to focus on the positive of the breakup. You can learn more about yourself and pour into yourself rather than focusing on someone and their happiness. Focus on yourself and making yourself happy.

❧ Pour into yourself and find out when you're ready and what you want for your future relationship.

❧ Think about what you want in the next relationship and become everything that you want from the other party. You are what you attract so it's time to become that!

❧   Being in a new relationship will not make you happy. Remember it starts with you and your healing before ever entering anything new.

Shana's

Boundaries & Standards

Boundaries are designed to keep your self-love intact and prevent you from being manipulated, used, or violated. This applies to dating, not once you start a committed relationship.

- ∽ **Discuss your communications styles-** from the start discuss your best ways to communicate with each other.

- ∽ **No last-minute dates - Discuss dates** - Be on the same page about future dates and locations so you both are on the same page. No last minute dates.

- ∽ **No calls after 11pm,** If we can't discuss things earlier than then I feel it can wait to the next day.

❧ **No Netflix and chill dates-** If you are dating me then, I feel like your time and money should be invested at least until things move forward. I love the Netflix and chill dates now lol.

❧ **No sex before a commitment –** I will not be pressed Into sex-based off how much someone spends on me or just because they're in the mood. If I feel we are committed or headed toward a commitment, then I will move according when it comes to sex.

❧ **I will not tolerate verbal abuse-** The way you start a relationship is how it will continue. Putting someone down or making them feel less than is not cool and I will not tolerate it at all.

I will not date someone who disrespects me in any way- If I respect you and do not call you outside your name our put you down, I expect the same always!

I will not chase anyone for love affection and or attention – If I must tell you how to treat me and date me then what is the point of having you. I want someone that isn't selfish and doesn't mind kissing me or holding my hand, just because, or bringing me flowers every blue moon just because and not just on holidays.

I will not pursue anyone who is not emotional ready for a relationship – If I am coming into this without any past hurts or baggage, I expect the same. If you're still hurting from a past relationship, traumatic experience or anything that will stop you from being emotionally ready to love me then you're not ready to date me or anyone for that matter.

❧ **I will not pay any bills for a man unless it's my husband or he has falling on hard times-** I have no issues helping someone out when they are at a bad place, but I will not do that unless he is my husband or someone, I see myself marrying. I need to know the ability of that man and his drive to get out of that space he is in

Standards are the qualities that must be present before you agree to entertain someone romantically.

- ✓ Must have the basics: job, own place, and able to support themselves.
- ✓ Someone who is family oriented and share the same morals and commitments as I do.
- ✓ Must be in a career they enjoy.
- ✓ No quick pop up and pop in and out dates
- ✓ No criminal record or drug use
- ✓ In a healthy state of mind Emotionally, physically, and financially
- ✓ Can identify and understand how to manage conflicts in any situation.
- ✓ Able to identify any issues that have and be willing to work on them.
- ✓ Willing to work on becoming and being the best version of themselves.

My SIDE NOTE FOR ALL TO REMEMBER:

Just because One relationship didn't work doesn't mean you give any less to the next relationship that comes into your life.

I NEVER gave up on a Man I was in a relationship with. I talked and talked to change and fix CERTAIN THINGS and when those things weren't changed or corrected, I simply left. Nobody is going to repeat themselves everyday nor are people going to wait forever to get what they DESERVE. The most selfish and manipulative thought process a person can have is to think you can treat people any kind of way and expect them to be there (saying that's love and loyalty), then when they leave you say they gave up on you. NO, you didn't apply yourself, for what you thought you was ready for. Keep it real or stay true with yourself, if nothing else keep it 💯 !! I will only address it so many times and that's because I cared, once I stop caring it's over!

168

*"Do unto others
as you would have them
do unto you!"*